F. SCOTT FITZGERALD

F. SCOTT FITZGERALD

A Biography

Edward J. Rielly

GREENWOOD BIOGRAPHIES

GREENWOOD PRESS
WESTPORT, CONNECTICUT · LONDON

Library of Congress Cataloging-in-Publication Data

Rielly, Edward J.
 F. Scott Fitzgerald: a biography / by Edward J. Rielly.
  p. cm. — (Greenwood biographies, ISSN 1540–4900)
 Includes bibliographical references and index.
 ISBN 0–313–33164–2 (alk. paper)
 1. Fitzgerald, F. Scott (Francis Scott), 1896–1940. 2. Authors,
American—20th century—Biography. I. Title. II. Series.
PS3511.I9Z829   2005
813'.52—dc22   2005020067

British Library Cataloguing in Publication Data is available.

Library of Congress Catalog Card Number: 2005020067
ISBN: 0–313–33164–2
ISSN: 1540–4900

First published in 2005

Greenwood Press, 88 Post Road West, Westport, CT 06881
An imprint of Greenwood Publishing Group, Inc.
www.greenwood.com

Printed in the United States of America

The paper used in this book complies with the
Permanent Paper Standard issued by the National
Information Standards Organization (Z39.48–1984).

10 9 8 7 6 5 4 3 2 1

CONTENTS

Photo essay follows page 56

SERIES FOREWORD

In response to high school and public library needs, Greenwood developed this distinguished series of full-length biographies specifically for student use. Prepared by field experts and professionals, these engaging biographies are tailored for high school students who need challenging yet accessible biographies. Ideal for secondary school assignments, the length, format, and subject areas are designed to meet educators' requirements and students' interests.

Greenwood offers an extensive selection of biographies spanning all curriculum-related subject areas including social studies, the sciences, literature and the arts, history and politics, as well as popular culture, covering public figures and famous personalities from all time periods and backgrounds, both historic and contemporary, who have made an impact on American and/or world culture. Greenwood biographies were chosen based on comprehensive feedback from librarians and educators. Consideration was given to both curriculum relevance and inherent interest. The result is an intriguing mix of the well known and the unexpected, the saints and sinners form long-ago history and contemporary pop culture. Readers will find a wide array of subject choices from fascinating crime figures like Al Capone to inspiring pioneers like Margaret Mead, from the greatest minds of our time like Stephen Hawking to the most amazing success stories of our day like J.K. Rowling.

While the emphasis is on fact, not glorification, the books are meant to be fun to read. Each volume provides in-depth information about the subject's life from birth through childhood, the teen years, and adulthood.

A thorough account relates family background and education, traces personal and professional influences, and explores struggles, accomplishments, and contributions. A timeline highlights the most significant life events against a historical perspective. Suggestions for further reading give the biographies added reference value.

ACKNOWLEDGMENTS

This book is written for students, so it is appropriate that I give special thanks to the thousands of students over the decades who have helped to make my life meaningful. Teaching is a chosen profession and a gift. I also thank those gifted teachers who taught and inspired me, especially Dr. Francis Lehner, now deceased, whose enthusiastic teaching of English to an uncertain Loras College freshman many years ago convinced that freshman to major in English, a decision I have never regretted. I also am deeply appreciative of the support given to me by my wife, Jeanne, and by the college where I teach, Saint Joseph's College of Maine.

INTRODUCTION

F. Scott Fitzgerald is a household name. Widely read in American high schools and colleges and in nations throughout the world, Fitzgerald is as American as apple pie. *The Great Gatsby* is his most famous novel, while many of his short stories—"Babylon Revisited," "Winter Dreams," "The Last of the Belles," "The Rich Boy," and "Bernice Bobs Her Hair" among others—are some of the best known and most widely read of American short stories.

It was not always so, and no one knew that, or perhaps cared more about it, than Fitzgerald himself. A self-consciously artistic writer, Fitzgerald aspired to literary greatness. He struck success early, while in his twenties, while the nation was also in its decade of the twenties within the twentieth century. Scott Fitzgerald and his wife, Zelda, embodied the exuberance and youthful vitality of the Jazz Age. Indeed, Fitzgerald is generally credited with giving the period that name. Who else can claim to have named a period in American history?

Unfortunately, Fitzgerald faced many obstacles to continued success and the ultimate realization of his dream, including his own alcoholism and his wife's mental illness. By the middle of the 1930s, Fitzgerald had fallen out of favor, partly because of changing literary tastes, but mainly because his own alcoholic and physical problems made writing an increasingly difficult challenge.

It did not help that Fitzgerald's status was seen (through his own eyes also) in juxtaposition with that of Ernest Hemingway, whom Fitzgerald had befriended in the 1920s when Hemingway was trying to break through as a writer of fiction and Fitzgerald already was a famous novelist. By the time Fitzgerald died in 1940, few people were reading his fiction, while Hemingway had achieved worldwide fame.

Yet Fitzgerald never gave up trying to reclaim his position in American letters. At the time of his death, he was working on a novel, *The Love of the Last Tycoon*, which likely would have helped him reclaim his proper place in the pantheon of great American writers. He died with the novel unfinished.

Nonetheless, a great rebirth of interest in Fitzgerald began to develop shortly after his death. That interest became like a great avalanche rushing down a mountain, and it has not yet stopped gathering up admirers—critic, student, and general reader alike. Some 65 years after Fitzgerald's death, his reputation is as secure as that of any other American author. Fitzgerald may have died in relative obscurity, but his fame appears likely to endure forever.

This book examines Fitzgerald's life and writings in a generally chronological way. It explains how his parents, markedly different in background, created opposing sets of values with which Fitzgerald struggled in childhood but later put to use in his fiction. Although most writers use material from their personal lives, Fitzgerald draws more heavily than most from his own personal experiences, using even some of his most painful moments to create memorable fiction.

Examining Fitzgerald's life, therefore, can shed considerable light on his novels and short stories. It also will help elucidate the creative process by which Fitzgerald borrowed raw materials for fiction from personal life and, through the creative functioning of his imagination, aided by careful attention to narrative and descriptive techniques, produced outstanding stories.

This biography also presents Fitzgerald within the context of his times, exploring, for example, how his life paralleled the decade of the 1920s, the Jazz Age, in their respective passages from high success to seemingly sudden crashes that, as the book notes, were not quite so sudden for either the author or the historical period.

Influences, such as Princeton University, which Fitzgerald attended but from which he never graduated, and sports, especially football, remained with Fitzgerald for life. Readers will find these influences discussed throughout the biography.

In addition, a variety of people who were immensely important to Fitzgerald appear within the following pages. There is his wife, Zelda, of course, who with her husband constituted the couple still today seen as the ultimate embodiment of the Jazz Age. The aforementioned Hemingway receives substantial treatment, befitting his position with Fitzgerald as one-half of one of the most famous literary friendships in the history of American literature. Old friends from Princeton, such as Edmund Wilson and Judge John Biggs, Jr.; Fitzgerald's editor at Scribners, Max Perkins; and his agent, Harold Ober, necessarily appear often.

Family conflicts, including the blame that Zelda's family assigned to Fitzgerald for his wife's mental illness, deeply affected him and also received fictional treatment within his writings. His love for his daughter, Scottie, comes through clearly in his life and writings, both fiction and letters. These matters also are important to a student of F. Scott Fitzgerald.

Finally, considerable attention is given to his final writing efforts, efforts perhaps deserving the epithet heroic, given the great difficulties under which he labored to carry them out; and to his death, which appeared to mark the end of a career but instead led to a great rebirth of a reputation. Fitzgerald wrote some of his best fiction, including his most widely read work, *The Great Gatsby,* about tragic heroes. In Fitzgerald's own life, tragedy was often present, much of it self-caused, but the conclusion of his personal story, so many decades later, seems more triumphant than tragic. Students of Fitzgerald's life and writings should consider how within an ending one sometimes can find a new beginning.

This biography of F. Scott Fitzgerald includes a variety of learning aids. One of them is a timeline, listing important events in Fitzgerald's life. Preparing a timeline is always challenging and necessarily somewhat subjective. How much should be included? Which details are most relevant? The compiler of such a timeline could end up virtually duplicating the entire biography in miniature, but instead has tried to offer a listing that should never be seen as a substitute for the biography but, perhaps more than anything, as a jog to memory and a means of keeping goings and comings straight.

The bibliography of Fitzgerald's published works has offered another challenge. Fitzgerald's life was cut short by death when he was not yet 44. Yet in his relatively short lifetime, much of it hindered by ailments associated with alcoholism, he succeeded in being truly prolific, a remarkable achievement in light of the difficulties he faced during the latter part of his life. So how much of this should appear here? To include a listing of every single story, review, essay, poem, and so forth, that he published would result in a voluminous cascade of works too daunting to be inviting and surely far more than any student would likely need.

Instead, the bibliography lists books in a reasonably thorough way, including anthologies compiled after his death. Screenplays also are noted. In addition, selected lists of individual story and essay publications are included, chosen for their special significance but also as illustrative of the whole. For example, the appendix includes a listing of the stories that appeared in *The Saturday Evening Post*, which was for much of Fitzgerald's career his primary short story market; and the late Pat Hobby stories that appeared in *Esquire* shortly before and after Fitzgerald's death. Also included are the "crack-up" essays that appeared in *Esquire* during the 1930s and that are related to important incidents involving Hemingway and a *New York Post* reporter, Michel Mok.

The "Secondary Sources" section is divided into four categories. Deciding whether a book belongs under "Selected Biographies and Memoirs" or "Selected Critical Works" may in some cases be somewhat subjective, as many biographical works, including this biography, also involve a great deal of critical discussion. Given the huge number of such books, it is possible to include only a sampling. Many useful works are left out in order to avoid an overly intimidating list. Nonetheless, a student will not go far wrong by beginning with some of these studies. No individual journal and magazine articles are included because the number is too massive and even a sampling seems of little help. In addition, most students, especially in high schools, but even in many colleges, will find it easier to locate books than journal articles. Selected Web sites also are listed, although readers should be reminded that online sites and addresses often change. Finally, biographical studies of some of Fitzgerald's friends offer additional opportunities for background research.

TIMELINE: EVENTS IN THE LIFE OF F. SCOTT FITZGERALD

1853   Edward Fitzgerald is born near Rockville, Maryland.

1860   Mary "Mollie" McQuillan is born in St. Paul, Minnesota.

1890   Marriage of Edward Fitzgerald and Mollie McQuillan.

1896   Frances Scott Key Fitzgerald is born in St. Paul on September 24.

1898   Fitzgerald family moves to Buffalo, New York, in April as Edward takes a position with Procter & Gamble.

1900   Birth of Zelda Sayre on July 24 in Montgomery, Alabama.

1901   Fitzgeralds move to Syracuse in January.

1901   Birth of FSF's sister, Annabel, on July 21.

1903   Fitzgeralds move back to Buffalo in September.

1908   Edward loses his job in March; Fitzgeralds return to St. Paul in July. In September, FSF enters St. Paul Academy.

1911   FSF enrolls at Newman School, Hackensack, New Jersey, in September.

1913   FSF enters Princeton in September.

1914   *Fie! Fie! Fi-Fi!*, book and lyrics by FSF, produced in December by Princeton's Triangle Club.

1915   FSF meets Ginevra King in January while home on vacation. In December, he drops out of Princeton for the rest of the academic year.

1916   FSF returns for his second junior year.

1917   First professional sale—a poem to *Poet Lore* in September. FSF is commissioned a Second Lieutenant in the army and reports to Fort Leavenworth, Kansas, for officer's training in November.

1918 FSF finishes first draft of *The Romantic Egotist*. While stationed at Camp Sheridan near Montgomery, meets Zelda Sayre in July. The manuscript is rejected by Scribners.

1919 FSF is discharged from the army in February; goes to New York to work for the Barron Collier advertising agency. Has his first commercial short story sale—"Babes in the Woods" to *The Smart Set*. Zelda breaks their engagement in June and FSF returns to St. Paul to rewrite his novel. Editor Max Perkins accepts *This Side of Paradise* for Scribners in September. In October FSF sells his first story to *The Saturday Evening Post* ("Heads and Shoulders"). Becomes a client of agent Harold Ober. Re-engaged to Zelda in November.

1920 *This Side of Paradise* published in March. FSF and Zelda are married in April and move to Westport, Connecticut. *Flappers and Philosophers* published in September. Fitzgeralds move to an apartment in New York City in October.

1921 In May the Fitzgeralds travel to Europe. In August they move to St. Paul to await the birth of their child, Frances Scott Fitzgerald (Scottie), born in October.

1922 *The Beautiful and Damned* and *Tales of the Jazz Age* published. Fitzgeralds move to Great Neck, Long Island, in October.

1923 *The Vegetable* fails at a tryout in Atlantic City.

1924 Fitzgeralds travel to Europe in May. Zelda'a involvement with Edouard Jozan occurs during the summer. Fitzgeralds become friends with Gerald and Sara Murphy.

1925 *The Great Gatsby* published. In May FSF meets Ernest Hemingway.

1926 *All the Sad Young Men* published. Fitzgeralds return to America in December.

1927 Fitzgeralds go to Hollywood where FSF writes the unproduced screenplay "Lipstick" and they meet Lois Moran. Fitzgeralds move to Ellerslie outside Wilmington, Delaware, in March.

1928 Fitzgeralds travel to Paris for the summer. Zelda begins ballet lessons with Lubov Egorova. In October they return to Ellerslie.

1929 Fitzgeralds return to Europe in March.

1930 In April Zelda suffers her first breakdown and enters Prangins Clinic in Switzerland in June.

1931 FSF visits America in January to attend the funeral of his father. Fitzgeralds return to Montgomery in September following Zelda's release from Prangins. In November FSF makes his second trip to Hollywood for screenwriting. Judge Anthony Sayre, Zelda's father, dies in November.

1932   Zelda's second breakdown occurs in January; she is admitted to Phipps Clinic of the Johns Hopkins Hospital, where she writes *Save Me the Waltz*. In May FSF rents La Paix near Baltimore. Zelda is discharged in June.

1933   Zelda's play *Scandalabra* produced in Baltimore June 26 to July 1. FSF publishes a memorial essay on Ring Lardner. Fitzgeralds rent a house on Park Avenue in Baltimore.

1934   *Tender Is the Night* published. Zelda is hospitalized at Sheppard-Pratt in May after her third breakdown.

1935   FSF is at Oak Hall Hotel in Tryon, North Carolina, in February. *Taps at Reveille* published in March. In May FSF moves to the Grove Park Inn, Asheville, North Carolina. In November he begins writing the Crack-Up essays at the Skyland Hotel in Hendersonville, North Carolina.

1936   The Crack-Up essays begin appearing in *Esquire;* Hemingway's "The Snows of Kilimanjaro" appears in the same magazine. In April, Zelda enters Highland Hospital in Asheville, North Carolina. FSF returns to the Grove Park Inn in July. In September, his mother dies, and he is interviewed by Michel Mok of the *New York Post*.

1937   FSF signs a six-month contract with Metro-Goldwyn-Mayer (MGM) and returns to Hollywood. He moves to the Garden of Allah Hotel in Hollywood and meets Sheilah Graham. *Three Comrades* provides his only screen credit. In December his contract is renewed for a year.

1938   FSF moves to Malibu Beach in April and to Encino in October. MGM declines to renew his contract.

1939   FSF works briefly on *Gone with the Wind*. In February he accompanies Budd Schulberg on a trip to Dartmouth College for work on *Winter Carnival*. FSF accompanies Zelda to Cuba in April. He breaks with Harold Ober in July.

1940   Publication in January of the first of seventeen Pat Hobby stories. Zelda is released from Highland Hospital in April and moves in with her mother in Montgomery. FSF moves to North Laurel Avenue, Hollywood, in May. In November he suffers a heart attack and moves in with Sheilah Graham. On December 21, FSF dies of a heart attack and is buried in Rockville Union Cemetery, Rockville, Maryland, on December 27.

1941   Publication of the unfinished *The Love of the Last Tycoon*.

1945   Publication of *The Crack-Up*.

1947   Zelda returns to Highland Hospital.
1948   Zelda dies in a fire at Highland Hospital on March 10 and is buried
        next to FSF on March 17.
1975   Scott and Zelda reinterred in the Fitzgerald family plot at St. Mary's
        Church, Rockville.

Chapter 1

THE EARLY YEARS: ST. PAUL AND NEWMAN SCHOOL (1896–1913)

Francis Scott Key Fitzgerald, who would become one of the great American authors of the twentieth century, was born on September 24, 1896, in St. Paul, Minnesota. Scott, the name he preferred to Francis, was a large, healthy baby, weighing 10 pounds, 6 ounces. The successful birth was a relief to his parents, Edward and Mary (Mollie) McQuillan Fitzgerald, who earlier in the year had lost their first two children, two girls aged one and three. A third daughter died within about an hour of her birth in 1900; a fourth, Annabel, born in 1901, survived. Annabel would marry Clifton Sprague, who, as Admiral Sprague, helped defeat the Japanese fleet in the Coral Sea in a critical World War II battle. She outlived her more famous brother by almost half a century, dying in 1987.

FAMILY BACKGROUND

Scott's parents were from markedly different backgrounds. Edward, born in 1853, was a Southerner who as a boy living behind Confederate lines in Rockville, Maryland, had helped Southern spies to escape detection by rowing them across a river. On Edward's mother's side, the family included both the famous and infamous: the ancestor after whom Scott was named, Francis Scott Key, author of "The Star-Spangled Banner"; and Mary Surratt, Edward's first cousin, who was hanged for her participation in the conspiracy to assassinate Abraham Lincoln. Edward attended Georgetown College (later University) without graduating and moved to Chicago and later St. Paul to try to make his fortune. In St. Paul in the late 1880s, he became proprietor of the American Rattan and

Willow Works, a small company that made furniture, and married Mollie McQuillan in 1890.

Mollie was the daughter of an Irish immigrant, Philip McQuillan, who arrived in the United States in 1843 at the age of nine, settled with his parents in Galena, Illinois, and then moved to St. Paul in 1857. In St. Paul, he quickly climbed the grocery ladder from bookkeeper to owner of his own grocery store, later becoming a grocery wholesaler whose warehouse was one of the largest buildings in the city. When Philip McQuillan died in 1877, he was one of the most prosperous businessmen in St. Paul, leaving his five surviving children, including Mollie, well provided for.

Mollie's money proved enormously helpful as Edward's furniture business failed in 1898. Edward found employment with Procter & Gamble as a wholesale grocery salesman, probably through the McQuillan connection, and moved his family to Buffalo, New York. The family moved often during Scott's childhood, not only from Buffalo to Syracuse, New York, in 1901 and back to Buffalo in 1903, but also within those cities, always renting. When Edward lost his position with Procter & Gamble in 1908, the Fitzgeralds returned to St. Paul, where the father, again assisted by his wife's family connections, secured a job as a wholesale grocery salesman, working out of a brother-in-law's real-estate office.

Young Scott reacted quite differently to his two parents. His father was a stylishly dressed man who took his son on Sundays to get their shoes polished, read Edgar Allan Poe and Lord Byron to Scott, told him stories of the Civil War, and praised his early writing efforts, including a Sherlock Holmes story. Edward's encouragement of his son's writing may reflect his own early writing ambitions. He once had co-authored an unpublished novel. Years later Scott, remembering that encouragement, credited his father with the first help he had ever received with his literary efforts.[1]

Scott saw in his father a representative of the Old South with its gentility, good manners, romance, and sense of history. At the same time, he came to feel strongly the financial failures of his father and the family's dependence on his mother's money. His father's financial reversals and the family's many moves created in Scott a sense of being an outsider, of being from a lower social and economic class than the children with whom he associated. This attitude of not quite belonging may at times have hindered his self-confidence, and it certainly caused him pain on occasion; nonetheless, this perceived status proved beneficial to the future writer. It contributed to his extraordinary capacity for being both within and without and thus closely observing what was happening around him even as he was an active participant in the event.

Mollie, feeling keenly the loss of three children, lavished attention on Scott and took him on trips with her. Thanks to her inherited money, she also provided him with educational privileges enjoyed by the moneyed and social elite. Yet despite his mother's best efforts, Scott often reacted negatively to her. He was embarrassed by her carelessness in dress and awkward manners. He also saw her as representative of the nouveau riche, a group relying on wealth and social pretensions rather than on the cultural "breeding"—if a lack of vitality—that he associated with his father.

This contrast between father and mother would emerge in Scott's fiction, such as the short story "The Ice Palace," with its contrasts between the North and South, money and romance, coldness and sensitivity toward others. Although Fitzgerald keenly felt his father's financial failings and aspired to what wealth could bring, he inevitably favored the values that he associated with his father over those he ascribed to his mother. The weakness and ineffectual quality that he perceived in his father did not lessen his sense of connection to the older man. Shortly after Edward Fitzgerald's death in 1931, Scott would remark in a letter that encountering Civil War references had awakened in him a sadness regarding his father and the past.[2]

While Edward Fitzgerald had encouraged in his son a reverence for the past, especially in relation to the South, and a love for literature that would be his avenue for escaping the personal futility that he associated with his father, his mother's contributions to Scott's intellectual and social development were of a more formal nature. Her determination that he receive a fine education, and her inheritance, led him to Miss Goodyear's School in the autumn of 1902. The following year, with the Fitzgeralds now back in Buffalo, Scott attended Holy Angels Convent. In 1905, he transferred to Miss Narden's and also attended Mr. Van Arnum's dance class.

By this time, Scott was establishing a mode of behavior that he would alternately practice and try to escape: boasting and showing off in order to establish himself not only as belonging with the children from greater money and social status than he, but also as a social leader. His active imagination and unhappiness with his perceived inferior status led to fantasies that he was not really the son of his supposed parents but had been deposited on their doorstep in infancy. In this daydream, he imagined himself of royal lineage, a fantasy that he later incorporated into the story "Absolution." Fitzgerald's Catholicism provided another early experience for the same story. His family's involvement with the Catholic Church in St. Paul was long-lived and substantial. Grandfather Philip McQuillan had contributed to the building of St. Mary's Church in 1866 and to importing from St. Louis the Sisters of the Visitation, whose school Scott's sister, Annabel, attended. With his parents both committed Catholics, Scott also followed traditional Catholic practices, including attending confession, now known as the rite of reconciliation. In one trip to the confessional, he inadvertently lied by unthinkingly assuring the priest that he never told lies, an event that he took seriously enough to make the incident in "Absolution" from which the entire story flows.

EARLY WRITING

Scott began to take writing seriously in Buffalo with such compositions as an essay on George Washington and Ignatius Loyola, an attempt at a history of the United States, detective stories, and plays. He also began to keep a "character book" in which he wrote his reactions to playmates, the beginning of a lifelong practice of meticulously recording his actions and thoughts, and later his publishing and financial history.

It was on his return to St. Paul in 1908, however, at St. Paul Academy, that Scott's literary and social aspirations came into clearer focus. His threefold preoccupations with sports, writing, and social status that dominated his St. Paul years would remain high priorities throughout much of his life.

Scott played end on the St. Paul football team and pitched for the baseball team, although on neither squad was he able to rise above second-team status. When he broke a rib playing football, the pain was significantly lessened by the pride he felt in being wounded on the field of play. Yale football star Ted Coy was one of his heroes, and in a story that Scott wrote while at St. Paul Academy, "Read, Substitute Right Half," he proved able to combine realistic self-assessment (the protagonist is small and only a substitute) with dramatic over-achievement. Read comes off the bench to lead his team to a come-from-behind victory.

"Read, Substitute Right Half" was Scott's second story to be published in his school newspaper, the St. Paul Academy Now and Then, appearing in the February 1910 issue. In the October 1909 issue, he had published "The Mystery of the Raymond Mortgage," an imitation of Edgar Allan Poe that was his first appearance in print. Two more of his stories appeared in Now and Then: "A Debt of Honor" (March 1910) and "The Room with the Green Blinds" (June 1911). These two final stories reflect Scott's continuing interest in the Confederacy as he writes, in the former, of a soldier who behaves heroically after falling asleep on duty and, in the latter, of John Wilkes Booth, the Abraham Lincoln assassin, who in

Scott's story escapes and lives for years in an old Southern mansion before finally being killed. Scott also began writing plays for the Elizabethan Dramatic Club, named after the club's founder, Elizabeth Magoffin, a woman in her early twenties from a prominent family in the prestigious Summit Avenue area of St. Paul. Her ancestors included two governors of Kentucky; the first governor of Massachusetts, Thomas Dudley; and the American statesman Henry Clay. Scott acted in a play called A *Regular Fix*, which was performed as a benefit for the Protestant Orphan Asylum, and in the summer of 1911, prior to his matriculation at Newman Academy, contributed *The Girl from Lazy J*. Performed less publicly, in the Magoffin home, *The Girl from Lazy J* is a brief romantic mystery set on a Texas ranch. Scott played the hero, Jack Darcy, who helps foil a robbery and gets the girl, Leticia, described in the play as "the prettiest girl this side of the Mississippi."[3]

The play offers little evidence of great literary potential, but it previews a theme important in Fitzgerald's later fiction, the young man winning the most beautiful and desirable girl. As Jack muses in the opening of the play, "Why, put her in a decent dress and she'd be the belle of the country."[4] Despite the modest quality of the play, Elizabeth Magoffin praised Scott highly, writing on a photograph that she gave her young playwright, "To Scott 'He had that Spark—Magnetic Mark—' With the best love of the one who thinks so." She also gave him a poem defining the spark as "a gift, and a part of our God."[5]

In addition to stories and plays, Scott continued the practice that he began in Buffalo of maintaining a written record of his activities. During 1910–11, he kept what he called a *Thoughtbook of Francis Scott Key Fitzgerald*. The *Thoughtbook* includes accounts of his romantic adventures and attempts to gain popularity, demonstrating Fitzgerald's willingness and acute ability to admit in writing to his deepest feelings and aspirations, an attitude that would continue in the "Crack-Up" essays of the 1930s, which chronicle his darkest doubts and deepest failures.

The desire to win the most beautiful girl, already expressed in *The Girl from Lazy J*, was an early element in Scott's desire for social supremacy, as well as in some of his early published stories, but he also desired the esteem of his male peers. In St. Paul, he was a member of Professor Baker's dancing class, which attracted boys and girls from prominent families, including Elizabeth "Betty" Ames, daughter of Charles Wilberforce Ames, president of West Publishing Company, in whose yard Scott, Betty, and friends spent many hours playing in a three-story tree house. At school, he tended to show off his intelligence and was quick with opinions, a trait that then and later got him into trouble. *Now and Then* in 1909 included the notice, "If anybody can poison Scotty or stop his mouth in some way, the school at large and myself will be obliged."[6] As with many moments from his childhood, even painful ones, this statement later appeared in a Fitzgerald short story, "The Freshest Boy."

Despite more than a little boasting, he made many friends in St. Paul and helped to organize a number of secret clubs that often met in the home of his friend Cecil Read. One of the clubs, the Scandal Detectives, devised a plan to embarrass another boy, Reuben Warner, who was especially popular with girls. The gambit supplied part of the plot for "The Scandal Detectives," the first in a series of eight short stories about the heavily autobiographical Basil Duke Lee published in the *Saturday Evening Post* in the late 1920s. A ninth story, "That Kind of Party," was rejected by the *Post,* apparently because it included children playing kissing games. Scott also enjoyed bob parties (which involved trips by horse-drawn wagons or sleds to the Town and Country Club for dance parties), spending time with Cecil Read at his parents' summer home at White Bear Lake, and attending summer camp at Frontenac, Minnesota.

These activities brought Scott into extensive interaction with children from the wealthy Summit Avenue neighborhood, an area of St. Paul that featured the luxuriant mansion owned by railroad tycoon James J. Hill, situated at 240 Summit Avenue. Fitzgerald later described Carl Miller, father of the protagonist, Rudolph, in the story "Absolution," as having only "two bonds with the colorful life"—"his faith in the Roman Catholic Church and his mystical worship of the Empire Builder, James J. Hill."[7] Scott regularly visited at the homes of his wealthier friends, but his parents, although residents of the Summit Avenue neighborhood, did not own a house. Instead, they rented a variety of apartments and homes, reinforcing Scott's sense of impoverishment and establishing a rootlessness that he would maintain as an adult, never living in the same place long and never owning his own home.

NEWMAN SCHOOL

Scott's parents decided to send him to the Newman School in Hackensack, New Jersey, for the 1911–12 academic year. As a prestigious Catholic prep school, it offered an opportunity for him to continue interacting with the sons of wealthy and socially prominent families, but it also, his parents hoped, would enforce greater academic discipline on their imaginative but often lazy and unmotivated son. The school was small (about sixty students) and only forty minutes from New York City, details that would impact both the new student and his later fiction.

In this small community, Scott may have thought that he could quickly translate his intelligence and charm into a position of leadership, but things did not work out as he hoped. Other students saw him, as many had at St. Paul Academy, as boastful and bossy, and when he ran away from a boy trying to tackle him in a football game, his schoolmates added cowardice to their tally of his failings. Scott's difficulties at Newman and his struggles to overcome his unpleasant start there receive vivid fictional treatment in "The Freshest Boy." The story is a touching account of the struggles of a boy ostracized by classmates and of his attempts to escape his unhappy setting, culminating in a trip to New York City to attend a play.

Scott's love for the theater, nurtured during his years at St. Paul Academy, blossomed further at Newman. His trips to New York helped him temporarily to escape the pain of his isolation; Scott especially enjoyed the performances of Ina Claire in *The Quaker Girl* and Gertrude Bryan in *Little Boy Blue*. Scott also continued writing plays for the Elizabethan Dramatic Club, contributing *The Captured Shadow* for a summer 1912 performance at Mrs. Backus's School for Girls in Oak Hall, with Scott playing the lead, a gentleman thief named Thornton Hart Dudley, also known as The Shadow. Dudley bets several New York men that he can prove the police incompetent by functioning uncaught as a burglar for two weeks. He successfully carries out the plan but returns everything that he steals, thus retaining his integrity. When he reaches the end of the two-week period, he admits his identity and purpose, at the same time winning the love of the beautiful Dorothy Connage.

The Captured Shadow, far superior to the earlier *The Girl from Lazy J*, was followed the next summer, after Scott's second and final year at Newman, by *Coward*. This drama marks a return to Fitzgerald's long-standing interest in the Civil War. Perhaps also drawing upon the playwright's early Newman misadventures at football, the play is about a Southerner, Jim Holworthy, who advances from coward to hero and winner of the hand of Lindy Douglas. The play was performed, with Scott doing double duty as Lieutenant Charles Douglas and Private Willings, as a benefit for the Baby Welfare Association at the St. Paul Y.W.C.A. on August 29, 1913, shortly before Scott left for Princeton University.

At Newman, Scott also wrote for the school magazine, the *Newman News*, contributing the poem "Football" and the short stories "A Luckless Santa Claus," "Pain and the Scientist," and "The Trail of the Duke."

Scott's second year was happier athletically and socially. Although never a great athlete, he contributed significantly to the football team's fortunes and was praised in the *Newman News* for a fine run against the Kingsley School squad that set up the winning touchdown by Charles W.

"Sap" Donahoe, who went to Princeton with Scott and remained a lifelong friend.

In addition to Scott's literary, social, and athletic adventures at Newman, his two years there included two other events that had lasting effects. During Easter vacation of his first year, he visited Cecilia "Ceci" Taylor, a cousin sixteen years his senior at whose wedding he had been a ribbon-holder. Ceci, the daughter of Edward Fitzgerald's sister, Eliza Delihant, lived in Norfolk, Virginia. An attractive and sensitive woman much admired by Scott, Ceci later appeared in Fitzgerald's first novel, *This Side of Paradise*, as Amory Blaine's cousin, the widowed Clara Page, "the first fine woman he ever knew and one of the few good people who ever interested him."[8] The description accurately reflects Scott's view of his cousin, with whom he maintained a warm and lasting relationship.

Scott also had a close relationship with Ceci's brother, Tom Delihant, a Jesuit priest, and visited him during the same Easter trip. Fitzgerald's daughter, Scottie, continued the relationship, with Fr. Delihant presiding at her marriage to Samuel "Jack" Lanahan in 1943 and baptizing their first child, Thomas "Tim" Lanahan, in 1946.[9] As with the visit to Ceci, his Easter 1913 reunion with Tom Delihant yielded fictional material, in this case for the short story "Benediction." An early version of the story, "The Ordeal," which Fitzgerald wrote at Princeton, presents a Jesuit's struggles regarding whether to take his final priestly vows and thus choose his "God-sense" over his "world-sense."[10]

The choice of a priestly vocation was on Scott's mind during his second year at Newman, in large measure because of his friendship with Father Cyril Sigourney Webster Fay, the model for Monsignor Darcy in *This Side of Paradise*. Scott first met Father Fay, a Newman trustee and later headmaster of the school, in November 1912 and was greatly impressed. Fay, a former Episcopalian minister, had converted to Catholicism and been ordained a priest. Wealthy and urbane, he had traveled extensively and numbered many influential people among his friends. Although overweight and not at all physically prepossessing, in fact appearing much older than his thirty-seven years, Fay charmed Scott with his erudition, sophistication, and ability to relate to the young, imaginative prep school student. Scott visited the priest several times in Washington, D.C., and found him attentive and respectful to his young visitor's ideas. Fay's idiosyncrasies, such as his fondness for elaborate liturgy and penchant for religious jokes, and the fact that, like Scott, he wrote poetry, helped cement the relationship. Father Fay joined Scott's father as the two people who most influenced his youth, but in Fay's case there was no accompanying sense of sadness over financial and social failure.

Among the people Scott met through Father Fay was Shane Leslie, an Anglo-Irish Catholic convert and sophisticated man of the world. A first cousin of Winston Churchill, the great World War II British prime minister, Leslie had been educated at some of England's finest institutions (Eton and King's College, Cambridge) and had known such literary luminaries as the Russian novelist Leo Tolstoy, the British poet and soldier Rupert Brooke (who died in 1915 during World War I), and the Irish poet William Butler Yeats.

Under the influence of Fay and Leslie, Scott saw Catholicism in a romantic light quite different from the faith of his parents and toyed with the idea of becoming a priest. The inclination toward a priestly vocation, though, was based primarily on Scott's perception of his two new friends and did not long survive his enrollment at Princeton University, which he had determined to attend for reasons only partly expressed in *This Side of Paradise*:

> Yale had a romance and glamour from the tales of Minneapolis, and St. Regis' men who had been "tapped for Skull and Bones," but Princeton drew him most, with its atmosphere of bright colors and its alluring reputation as the pleasantest country club in America.[11]

Princeton's Triangle Club, which produced an annual musical comedy, and the excitement of Princeton athletics also drew Scott. Hobey Baker, a football and hockey star, was one of his heroes. The death of Scott's Grandmother McQuillan in the summer of 1913 ensured sufficient funds for college tuition, and by the end of summer, he was looking forward to the next phase of his life and to the social, athletic, and literary achievements that he expected to be part of his future.

NOTES

1. *Correspondence of F. Scott Fitzgerald,* ed. Matthew J. Bruccoli and Margaret M. Duggan, with Susan Walker (New York: Random House, 1980), 322.

2. *Correspondence,* 261.

3. *F. Scott Fitzgerald's St. Paul Plays 1911–1914,* ed. Alan Margolies (Princeton, NJ: Princeton University Library, 1978), 15.

4. *St. Paul Plays,* 15.

5. Margolies, Introduction, *St. Paul Plays,* 4.

6. Matthew J. Bruccoli, *Some Sort of Epic Grandeur: The Life of F. Scott Fitzgerald,* 2nd rev. ed. (Columbia: University of South Carolina Press, 2002), 23.

7. F. Scott Fitzgerald, "Absolution," in *The Short Stories of F. Scott Fitzgerald,* ed. Matthew J. Bruccoli (1989; New York: Simon and Schuster, 1995), 264.

For a biography of Hill, see Albro Martin, *James J. Hill and the Opening of the Northwest* (1976; St. Paul: Minnesota Historical Society Press, 1991).

8. F. Scott Fitzgerald, *This Side of Paradise* (1920; New York: Scribners, 2003), 133.

9. Eleanor Lanahan, *Scottie, the Daughter of . . .: The Life of Frances Scott Fitzgerald Lanahan Smith* (New York: HarperCollins, 1995), 150–75.

10. F. Scott Fitzgerald, "The Ordeal," in *The Princeton Years: Selected Writing, 1914–1920*, ed. Chip Deffaa (Fort Bragg, CA: Cypress House, 1996), 35.

11. *This Side of Paradise*, 41.

Chapter 2

PRINCETON UNIVERSITY: PROMISE AND DISAPPOINTMENT (1913–1917)

F. Scott Fitzgerald entered Princeton University in the fall of 1913. Princeton then was primarily an undergraduate college with an enrollment of about 1,500 students. It boasted as a former president Woodrow Wilson, who had gone on to the governorship of New Jersey and, during Fitzgerald's years at Princeton, the presidency of the United States.

Fitzgerald's spotty academic performance at Newman School (where he had failed four courses—Algebra I, Caesar, French B, and Physics) led to his being admitted with conditions in those four areas (algebra, Latin, French, and physics), which had to be met with make-up exams. Matriculating with conditions was not unusual, as roughly two-thirds of Fitzgerald's freshman class entered with one or more.[1] However, Fitzgerald also had to make a personal plea for admittance. Unfortunately, he did not take his precarious academic status seriously enough. His aspirations being more athletic and social than academic, he was more concerned with his football future than with remedying academic deficiencies, wiring his parents, after receiving word of his acceptance, to send his football pads and shoes.

Even by early twentieth-century standards, Fitzgerald, at five foot seven and 138 pounds, was small for football. By comparison, Hobey Baker, a senior at Princeton during Fitzgerald's freshman year and probably the greatest all-around athlete of his time, was five foot nine and 160 pounds.[2] Baker, a Fitzgerald hero, became the model for Allenby, the football captain in *This Side of Paradise*. Fitzgerald, however, did not last long on the gridiron, according to conflicting accounts either the victim of a knee injury or cut from the team for lack of ability.

LITERARY SUCCESSES AND LOVE

The disappointed freshman quickly turned to other avenues for acceptance, going out for the Triangle Club, which sponsored an annual musical comedy that toured the country over Christmas break, and the *Princeton Tiger*, the college's humor magazine. He also embarked upon friendships that in many cases would last his entire life. Charles W. "Sap" Donahoe, a Newman classmate, shared 15 University Place with Fitzgerald and remained a lifelong friend. John Peale Bishop, the model for Thomas Park D'Invilliers in *This Side of Paradise*, and Fitzgerald engaged in extensive discussions of poetry, with Bishop something of a poetry mentor for Fitzgerald. Another enduring influence on him was Edmund "Bunny" Wilson, a year ahead of Fitzgerald at Princeton and a member of the *Nassau Literary Magazine* staff. Bishop became a successful poet, novelist, and reviewer, while Wilson established himself as one of the leading literary critics and magazine editors of the century. Each was managing editor of *Vanity Fair* for a time, with Wilson also serving as associate editor of *The New Republic*. Bishop later would write "The Hours," a poetic elegy on Fitzgerald's death; and Wilson, who survived both, after their deaths edited Bishop's collected essays, Fitzgerald's unfinished novel, *The Last Tycoon*, and a collection of Fitzgerald's autobiographical writings and tributes to Fitzgerald called *The Crack-Up*.

Fitzgerald retained his fascination with football, attending the Princeton-Yale game at New Haven, which ended in a 3–3 tie with Hobey Baker providing Princeton's lone score on a forty-three-yard drop-kick field goal. Fitzgerald scored his own goal in a different setting with his book and lyrics for *Fie! Fie! Fi-Fi!*, which was selected as the Triangle Club production for the following year, the author to play the role of the dancer Celeste in the all-male cast. He also expanded his literary interests, finding such writers as Robert Hugh Benson, H. G. Wells, George Bernard Shaw, and Compton Mackenzie especially inspiring. One of his favorite books was Mackenzie's two-volume novel *Sinister Street*, its plot about a young man's spiritual journey leading finally to the life of a priest resonating with Fitzgerald's own spiritual quest embodied in his friendship with Father Fay.

Fitzgerald's enthusiasm for writing and reading did not translate into academic success. His grade-point average for the first term was 5.17 in a seven-group system in which first through third groups roughly paralleled modern grades A through C, with groups four and five both indicating below average work and the final two groups unsatisfactory performance. His grade average would approximate something in the D range today. He had to take the exam in hygiene twice and the trigonometry and algebra exams three times in order to pass those three courses. His best grade was a 4 in English, still below average. Second-term results were little better. He managed a 3 (or satisfactory) in English but failed coordinate geometry.[3] He considered most of his professors dull and had great difficulty motivating himself to expend much effort in his courses.

After his freshman year, Fitzgerald spent the summer back in St. Paul. He wrote a final play, *Assorted Spirits*, for the Elizabethan Dramatic Club, also acting in it and serving as stage manager. A complicated plot that included a man dressing as a devil and haunting a house in order to get a good deal on it, a female burglar, a fortune teller, and a variety of romantic relationships did not cloak its considerable humor when performed at the Y.W.C.A. and the White Bear Yacht Club.[4]

Fitzgerald's sophomore year offered what he considered his greatest achievements at Princeton, but the year was not without its difficulties. He began by failing his make-up exam in coordinate geometry, thus becoming ineligible for extracurricular activities. As a result, he was not able to appear in the production of *Fie! Fie! Fi-Fi!* when it went on its Christmas tour. Instead, Fitzgerald returned home for the holidays, finding recompense for his inability to accompany the tour in his first great love.

She was Ginevra King, an attractive, wealthy socialite from a prominent Lake Forest, Illinois, family. Ginevra was visiting St. Paul as the guest of Marie Hersey, a neighborhood friend of Fitzgerald's and roommate of Ginevra's at Westover School in Connecticut. Ginevra embodied Fitzgerald's feminine ideal: a beautiful, socially confident, and popular girl who proved her value through her desirability. Such women would become a popular type in Fitzgerald's fiction, appearing in many incarnations, including Judy Jones in "Winter Dreams" and Daisy Buchanan in *The Great Gatsby*.

Romantic relationships were not only important to Fitzgerald but also the subject of much personal introspection. As Fitzgerald recorded in his *Notebooks*, he prided himself on his "good looks and intelligence"[5]; he also devoted considerable thought to the concept of the good "line," that is, witty repartee designed to interest a member of the opposite sex in the speaker. During his college years, Fitzgerald shared his insights regarding effective lines in a lengthy letter to his sister, Annabel, offering her a program of dress, speech, and action designed to make her socially confident.[6] The letter became the basis for the story "Bernice Bobs Her Hair," in which Bernice's line about getting her hair bobbed gets her into considerable trouble.

Despite Fitzgerald's self-appraisal, which might imply the ability to maintain the dominant position in relationships, he quickly became enthralled with Ginevra, writing her lengthy letters, sometimes several pages long, after his return to Princeton. At the end of the academic year, Ginevra came down to Princeton for the prom and a visit to New York with Fitzgerald to see the play *Nobody Home* and visit the Midnight Frolic Cabaret. On his way home for the summer break, he stopped at Lake Forest for a visit.

In the meantime, much was happening for Fitzgerald. He wrote for the *Princeton Tiger* and the *Nassau Literary Magazine*, contributing to the latter a one-act play, *Shadow Laurels,* which drew upon his ambivalent attitudes toward his father, and the story "The Ordeal." With Edmund Wilson writing the book, he composed the lyrics for *The Evil Eye,* selected as the Triangle Club production for the following year.

SOCIAL TRIUMPHS

In February, Fitzgerald was elected secretary of the Triangle Club, which put him in line to become the club's president in his senior year. In addition, he was invited to join the Cottage Club, one of the most prestigious of the Princeton eating clubs that served a social role similar to fraternities at other universities and which Woodrow Wilson had tried to abolish. Although Quadrangle was generally the favorite of literary types, Fitzgerald preferred Cottage, which he considered the haven for the Princeton gentleman. Celebrating his election to Cottage at the club's welcoming party, he drank heavily enough to pass out, apparently the first time he had undergone that experience. He also was chosen for the editorial board of *The Tiger*.

There remained, however, the matter of grades. Although Fitzgerald passed five of his six courses during the fall term, he was required to take seven courses in the second term, including coordinate geometry, which he had previously failed, and a course to compensate for excessive first-term absences. The results at the end of the second term declined sharply. He initially passed only four of the seven courses, finally passing two more on repeat exams, with qualitative analysis, a chemistry course, resisting three attempts at mastering the final exam.

After returning briefly to St. Paul in the summer, Fitzgerald traveled to Montana to spend some time with Sap Donahoe, who had entered Cottage with Fitzgerald, on the Donahoe ranch in White Sulphur Springs, located in south central Montana north of Bozeman. The visit supplied the basis for Fitzgerald's story "The Diamond as Big as the Ritz." Although there is no record of the amount of sightseeing that Fitzgerald did there, a number of local scenes as well as local history are echoed in the story, including the impressive nearby Big Belt, Little Belt, and Castle Mountains (collectively giving the area the nickname "Land of the Shining Mountains") and the area's mining history. Most of the mining had been for gold or silver, but a nearby ghost town named Diamond City had once been seat of Meagher County, in which White Sulphur Springs is located. An impressive gray limestone building known as The Castle, built by stockman and mine owner B. R. Sherman and located on top of a hill, may well have served as the model for the Washington chateau.

FAILED DREAMS

Fitzgerald returned to Princeton for his junior year on the cusp of becoming, as he wrote in *This Side of Paradise*, "a power in college."[7] Quickly, however, his dreams broke up on the hard rocks of academic failure. He failed a make-up exam in qualitative analysis and was declared ineligible for campus offices, including the Triangle Club presidency. Almost twenty years later, Fitzgerald wrote of this moment at a time when he was experiencing a welter of personal misfortunes that had led to what he called his "dark night of the soul."[8] In this later essay, "Handle with Care," he recalled only two previous instances of such disappointment and despair: when Zelda had broken off their engagement and, before that, the collapse of Fitzgerald's college dreams. As he wrote: "To me college would never be the same. There were to be no badges of pride, no medals, after all. It seemed on one March afternoon that I had lost every single thing I wanted—and that night was the first time that I hunted down the spectre of womanhood that, for a little while, makes everything else seem unimportant."[9] That Fitzgerald found solace in an anonymous sexual encounter testifies to how traumatic he found his university failures. Then and throughout his life, Fitzgerald was generally conservative in his attitude toward sex. His romantic view of love also tended to idealize women even as he recognized their individual faults. Neither attitude encouraged casual sex.

A story that Fitzgerald wrote at Princeton, "Sentiment—And the Use of Rouge," conveys his conventional view of premarital sex. Lieutenant Clay Harrington Syneforth, a British soldier home on leave from World War I, encounters his dead brother's former girlfriend, Eleanor Marbrooke, at a dance. She invites herself back to Syneforth's apartment, and, with great reluctance, he acquiesces. Eleanor mocks his concern that her presence in his apartment might compromise her, and finally Syneforth yields to temptation. The next day he is shocked when she explains that women have routinely been sleeping with their soldier-boyfriends before they go off to war: "Young men are going to get killed for us.—We would have been their wives—we can't be—therefore we'll be as much as we can. And that's the story." "Good God! he exclaims"[10] Clay Syneforth later writes to Eleanor, doing what he considers his duty, which is to urge marriage. Ever the more unconventional figure, the woman refuses, leaving the soon-to-be-dead soldier to worry whether his young sister, Clara, "was still well—virtuous."[11]

One of the few highlights of the year for Fitzgerald was the course in French literature that he took with Christian Gauss. Unlike his attitude toward most Princeton professors, Fitzgerald admired Gauss and remained close to him after leaving Princeton, exchanging letters a number of times during the 1920s and 1930s. In 1934, for example, Gauss wrote urging Fitzgerald to address The Club, an organization of Princeton undergraduates interested in creative literature. The next year Fitzgerald wrote his former professor requesting a selection of old French tests that his daughter, Scottie, could use to improve her French grammar. Gauss quickly complied, sending off a bundle of exams.[12]

Ineligible to act in *The Evil Eye,* Fitzgerald nonetheless helped with production of the musical and was photographed as a showgirl to publicize the all-male play. Among his writings that year was the winning entry in the competition for a new Princeton football song—"A Cheer for Princeton."

Not much else went right for him, though, and illness added to his other misfortunes. He twice was diagnosed with malaria and forced to spend time in the university infirmary. Fitzgerald later said that an X ray showed he instead had suffered a mild case of tuberculosis. Faced that fall with the probability of dismissal for academic reasons, Fitzgerald left Princeton at the end of November to recuperate, persuading Dean Howard McClennan to write a letter stating that he had withdrawn voluntarily for health reasons. Fitzgerald's official transcript, however, showed that he had been required to leave because of his academic performance.[13]

The year 1915–16 was not a good one for Ginevra King either. She was expelled from Westover in March, an action that deeply disturbed Fitzgerald. He later used the incident as a cautionary example for his daughter.[14]

A SECOND JUNIOR YEAR

Fitzgerald returned to Princeton in the fall of 1916 for his second attempt at a junior year but felt he was treading water. Deprived of his offices and status as a college power, and with his relationship with Ginevra King deteriorating, he nonetheless made the year a productive one in terms of his writing. As a future novelist and short-story writer, this year would prove his best at Princeton, although he clearly did not view it that way at the time.

Fitzgerald wrote the lyrics for the 1916–17 Triangle Club production, *Safety First*. John Biggs, Jr., who had entered Princeton a year after Fitzgerald but was now a classmate of his, wrote the book for the musical. The two would room together the following year and remained lifelong friends, Biggs serving as the executor of Fitzgerald's will. Biggs later published two novels and wrote several others but achieved his greatest success as a judge. He was named by President Franklin D. Roosevelt to the U.S. Court of Appeals for the Third Circuit (with jurisdiction in Pennsylvania, New Jersey, Delaware, and the Virgin Islands) in 1937. Two years later, Biggs became chief judge of the Third Circuit. Perhaps his most significant case occurred during the 1950s in *Schempp v. School District of Abington Township*. In *Schempp*, Biggs and his two colleagues on the court declared unconstitutional a Pennsylvania statute requiring Bible readings in public schools, a position affirmed by the U.S. Supreme Court in 1963.[15]

Fitzgerald published several stories that year in the *Nassau Literary Magazine*. Collectively, they show a young writer developing his ability to tell a nuanced story that, while portraying young men and women, does so in a mature manner. Several of Fitzgerald's junior-year writings would be published again, in some cases incorporated into his first novel, *This Side of Paradise*.

"Jemina: A Story of the Blue Ridge Mountains," published under the pseudonym John Phlox, Jr., parodies the fiction of popular author John Fox, Jr. Although much less substantial than several of his other stories of the year, it appealed sufficiently to its author to be included with a new subtitle in the short-story collection *Tales of the Jazz Age*, which appeared in 1922, the same year in which Fitzgerald's second novel, *The Beautiful and Damned*, was published.

"The Spire and the Gargoyle" uses those aspects of the Gothic architecture of Princeton's buildings mentioned in the title to symbolize, respectively, the protagonist's (and the author's) university aspirations and those university faculty whose insensitive demands blighted the potential of young creative minds:

> In view of his window a tower sprang upward, grew into a spire, yearning higher till its uppermost end was half invisible against the morning skies. The transiency and relative unimportance of the campus figures except as holders of a sort of apostolic succession had first impressed themselves on him in contrast with this spire. In a lecture or in an article or in conversation, he had learned that Gothic

architecture with its upward trend was peculiarly adapted to colleges, and the symbolism of this idea had become personal to him.[16]

By contrast, the preceptor who administers the test that the main character fails, leading to his forced departure from Princeton, reminds him of a gargoyle.[17]

Later the former Princeton student, who now realizes his own culpability for failing out of Princeton, encounters the preceptor after he has been forced to leave the university for a better paying job teaching in a Brooklyn high school. The ex-student meets the former preceptor again as both are returning to the university, the latter to visit his brother on the Princeton faculty, the former to visit the place to which he still has a strong emotional attachment. As the failed student steps off the train, though, he looks toward the university buildings, now shrouded partly in mist, strains to see the spire, and recognizes his inability to climb it.[18] Dejectedly, feeling "no injustice, only a deep mute longing," he picks up his suitcase and carries it back to the train.[19] Passages in the story describing the spire and other inspiring aspects of Princeton's Gothic architecture would reappear in *This Side of Paradise*.[20]

Fitzgerald's own failure to graduate from Princeton was one of his greatest personal disappointments. Yet despite that disappointment, Fitzgerald retained a lifelong fondness for Princeton, revisiting occasionally and avidly following news of the university, including the fortunes of its football team. At the moment of his death approximately twenty-three years after the end of his university days, he was making notes on Princeton's latest football team in a copy of the *Princeton Alumni Weekly*.

"Tarquin of Cheepside," another *Nassau Literary Magazine* story, presents a fictional version of how Shakespeare wrote the poem "The Rape of Lucrece" and, with the spelling corrected to "Cheapside," reappeared in *Tales of the Jazz Age*. The misspelling was not unusual for Fitzgerald, who remained a notoriously bad speller all his life.

"Babes in the Woods" is based on Fitzgerald's meeting with Ginevra King in St. Paul and later became both its author's first commercial sale of a story (to *The Smart Set* in 1920) and the description in *This Side of Paradise* of Amory Blaine's first encounter with Isabelle.[21] As Fitzgerald's romance with Ginevra King faltered, he turned to his writing to analyze the relationship. Along with "Babes in the Woods," a short play entitled *The Debutante* also was based on Ginevra King, published in the *Nassau Literary Magazine*, and revised for use in Fitzgerald's first novel.[22]

Also among the large literary output of Fitzgerald's second junior year are the aforementioned story "Sentiment—And the Use of Rouge" and the poem "Princeton—The Last Day," later incorporated in a prose version into *This Side of Paradise* to conclude book 1, "The Romantic Egotist."[23] Fitzgerald was a competent poet, but his talents lay much more in fiction than in poetry. His primary poetic influence was John Keats, whose use of rich descriptions, including synesthesia (the depiction of one type of sensory impression in terms usually associated with another sense), influenced Fitzgerald's prose style.

Academically, Fitzgerald continued to struggle, his first-term grades falling into extremes. He failed three courses (history, chemistry, and philosophy) but also earned his two highest grades at Princeton, a 2, analogous to a B, in English Renaissance poetry and in Christian Gauss's course on French romantic literature.

During the 1916–17 academic year, an anti-club student movement developed at Princeton. Fitzgerald, who had so delighted in his membership in the Cottage Club, did not support the movement but was friends with several prominent members of it, including David K.E. Bruce and Henry Strater. Bruce, whose father was a U.S. senator from Maryland and Pulitzer Prize winner for a book on Benjamin Franklin,[24] left Princeton after a year and a half for World War I. He later served Presidents Truman, Eisenhower, Kennedy, and Johnson in a variety of positions, including U.S. Ambassador to France (1949–52), Ambassador to Great Britain (1961–69), and chief of the U.S. delegation to the Paris Peace Conference on Vietnam (1970–71). Strater also enlisted in the war effort, serving as an ambulance driver, and later became a prominent artist whose paintings included three portraits of Ernest Hemingway. Strater also founded an art museum, the Ogunquit Museum of American Art, in Ogunquit, Maine.

WORLD WAR I

The United States entered the war on April 6, 1917. As with large numbers of young men throughout the country, Fitzgerald signed up for military training. Under the plan developed for college students, Fitzgerald would receive credit for courses dropped in order to carry out the training. Ironically, Fitzgerald earned his best grades of his university career for the term, automatically receiving a passing grade of 3 for each of his courses.

At the conclusion of the year, Fitzgerald returned to St. Paul, where he took the exam for an infantry commission while also seriously considering an invitation from Father Fay, with whom he had remained close since Newman, to accompany the churchman on a secret mission to Russia to unify the Catholic Church. Fitzgerald dutifully secured his passport and moved forward with plans for the trip. However, with Russia in turmoil as a result of the communist revolution, the mission was canceled. Fay instead went to Rome on behalf of the Red Cross and, increasingly recognized as a rising figure in the Catholic Church, received the priestly title and office of monsignor.

Fitzgerald returned to Princeton in the fall of 1917 for his fifth year, waiting for his military orders to come through. In the meantime, he continued writing, securing his first acceptance by a noncollege publication when *Poet Lore* took his poem "The Way of Purgation," although the poem was not published. He also continued writing fiction, contributing "The Pierian Springs and the Last Straw" to *The Nassau Lit*. The story includes a character type that would reappear later, the beautiful and thoroughly desirable woman who goes directly after what she wants regardless of the consequences to others; another character in the story calls the woman "the most direct, unprincipled personality I've ever come in contact with."[25] Almost those same words reappear in "Winter Dreams" to describe Judy Jones.[26]

The anticipated commission as a second lieutenant finally came through on October 26, 1917, and Fitzgerald was on his way to the next chapter in his life. It would include another great disappointment but also a meeting that would change his life.

NOTES

1. Matthew J. Bruccoli, *Some Sort of Epic Grandeur: The Life of F. Scott Fitzgerald*, 2nd rev. ed. (Columbia: University of South Carolina Press, 2002), 41.

2. John Davies, *The Legend of Hobey Baker* (Boston: Little, Brown, 1966), 19.

3. Bruccoli, *Some Sort of Epic Grandeur*, 43–44, 49.

4. *F. Scott Fitzgerald's St. Paul Plays 1911–1914*, ed. Alan Margolies (Princeton, NJ: Princeton University Library, 1978), 89.

5. *The Notebooks of F. Scott Fitzgerald*, ed. Matthew J. Bruccoli (New York: Harcourt Brace Jovanovich, 1980), entry 1378.

6. *Correspondence of F. Scott Fitzgerald*, ed. Matthew J. Bruccoli and Margaret M. Duggan, with Susan Walker (New York: Random House, 1980), 15–18.

7. F. Scott Fitzgerald, *This Side of Paradise* (1920; New York: Scribners, 2003), 96.

8. *The Crack-Up*, ed. Edmund Wilson (1945; New York: New Directions, 1956), 75.

9. Ibid., 76.

10. *The Princeton Years: Selected Writings, 1914–1920*, ed. Chip Deffaa (Fort Bragg, CA: Cypress House, 1996), 127.

11. Ibid., 128.

12. For correspondence between Gauss and Fitzgerald as well as other writings by Gauss, see *The Papers of Christian Gauss,* ed. Katherine Gauss Jackson and Hiram Haydn (New York: Random House, 1957).

13. Bruccoli, *Some Sort of Epic Grandeur,* 60.

14. F. Scott Fitzgerald, *Letters to His Daughter,* ed. Andrew Turnbull (New York: Scribners, 1965), 23.

15. For an extensive examination of John Biggs's life and career, see Seymour I. Toll, *A Judge Uncommon: A Life of John Biggs, Jr.* (Philadelphia: Legal Communications, 1993).

16. *The Princeton Years,* 90.

17. Ibid.

18. Ibid., 93.

19. Ibid.

20. *This Side of Paradise,* 57–58.

21. Ibid., 63–72.

22. Ibid., 157–69.

23. Ibid., 145.

24. William Cabell Bruce won a 1918 Pulitzer Prize for *Benjamin Franklin, Self-Revealed; a Biographical and Critical Study Based Mainly on His Own Writings* (New York: G. P. Putnam's Sons, 1917).

25. *The Princeton Years,* 144.

26. F. Scott Fitzgerald, "Winter Dreams," in *The Short Stories of F. Scott Fitzgerald,* ed. Matthew J. Bruccoli (1989; New York: Simon and Schuster, 1995), 226.

Chapter 3

WAR AND LOVE: ZELDA, THE DREAM GIRL (1917–1920)

F. Scott Fitzgerald's commission as a second lieutenant, dated October 26, 1917, arrived, ending his university career and opening up, so Fitzgerald thought, the possibility of heroism on foreign shores. Like so many other young men heading off to war, he imagined a glorious death on the battlefield and his heroic exploits living on in the nation's memory. Several wars later, that attitude sounds naïve, even incredible, but it reflected the high sense of patriotism and romanticism that motivated Fitzgerald and other war-bound men who, of course, had little knowledge of the horrors of trench warfare, mustard gas, and no-man's lands that awaited America's soldiers.

The realization that he might well be heading for an early death was a strong motivating factor behind the great energy Fitzgerald put into attempting to complete his first, and he feared, final, novel. The effort would take up much of his spare time during military training.

Fitzgerald's first stop on his presumed path to Europe was Brooks Brothers in New York, an elegant supplier of men's wear, where he purchased his army uniform. Uniforms then were neither standardized nor automatically supplied by the army. Stylishly outfitted, he reported to Fort Leavenworth, Kansas, where his training platoon was headed by Captain Dwight D. Eisenhower, later chief architect of D-Day in World War II and, still later, president of the United States.

A FIRST NOVEL

Considered by some who knew him then the worst soldier they ever saw, Fitzgerald worked assiduously on his manuscript, more interested in finishing the novel than perfecting his military talents. He used a leave in late February to complete the novel on a return trip to the Cottage Club at Princeton. Fitzgerald sent the manuscript to Shane Leslie, whom he had met through Monsignor Fay and who had agreed to submit it to his own publisher, Charles Scribner's Sons.

Leslie tidied up some of the spelling and grammar before forwarding the manuscript, entitled *The Romantic Egotist,* to Charles Scribner with a cover letter that was more like a critical analysis than an unqualified endorsement:

> In spite of its disguises, it has given me a vivid picture of the American generation that is hastening to war. I marvel at its crudity and its cleverness. It is naïve in places, shocking in others, painful to the conventional and not without a touch of ironic sublimity especially toward the end. About a third of the book could be omitted without losing the impression that it is written by an American Rupert Brooke.[1]

The submission made the rounds of several editors at the publishing house without a positive reaction until it reached Maxwell Perkins, who, alone among the Scribners editors, was impressed. Perkins responded to Fitzgerald, declining to publish but inviting resubmission after the author had revised the manuscript. He especially urged Fitzgerald to develop more of a definite conclusion. His letter, dated August 19, 1918, and written in the first person plural, conveyed his own enthusiasm for the work, especially its originality, but hid the general distaste felt by the rest of the editorial staff of the highly regarded but conservative firm.[2]

By this time, Fitzgerald had been transferred three times: to Camp Zachary Taylor, near Louisville, Kentucky (where Jay Gatsby of Fitzgerald's third novel also will be stationed and meet Daisy Fay); Camp Gordon, Georgia; and, finally, in June, 1918, Camp Sheridan, near Montgomery, Alabama, where despite his general incompetence as a soldier he was promoted to first lieutenant.

ZELDA SAYRE, THE BELLE OF THE BALL

At Montgomery, Fitzgerald met the woman who would become both purpose and subject for much of his writing, Zelda Sayre. One Saturday evening in July, a few weeks after receiving news of Ginevra King's engagement, Fitzgerald saw an attractive young woman with golden hair and blue eyes dancing with one of his friends, Major Dana Palmer. Immediately after the dance, he asked Palmer to introduce him to the woman.

Zelda, born on July 24, 1900, was the youngest of five surviving children (four daughters and one son, another boy, Daniel, having died young) in the Sayre household. The father, Anthony Dickinson Sayre, already sixty in 1918, was a member of the Alabama State Supreme Court. His mother's brother was Alabama U.S. Senator John Tyler Morgan, a brigadier general in the Confederate army who served in the Senate from 1876 until his death in 1907. Zelda often rebelled against her austere and serious father but until his death in 1931 psychologically depended on him as a bulwark of stability in her life.

Zelda's mother, Minerva "Minnie" Machen Sayre, also came from a distinguished family, her father, Willis B. Machen, having served in the First and Second Confederate Congresses and later in the U.S. Senate (1872–73), appointed to complete the term of the deceased Garrett Davis.

Zelda was beautiful, popular, and unconventional. With Montgomery overflowing with young soldiers on their way overseas, Zelda was the belle of the ball. It was said that aviators buzzed her home to impress her. Her popularity, in Fitzgerald's eyes, rendered her all the more desirable, although he also would suffer from periodic jealousy.

Zelda was a woman of two cultures: the traditional, genteel culture of the Old South; and the world of the new woman of ambition, independence, and iconoclasm. What Sally Carrol Happer says of herself in Fitzgerald's story "The Ice Palace" was also true of Zelda: "There's two sides to me, you see. There's the sleepy old side you love; an' there's a sort of energy—the feelin' that makes me do wild things. That's the part of me that may be useful somewhere, that'll last when I'm not beautiful any more."[3] Zelda was too complex of a person to be explained by a general designation, such as "flapper," a character type of the 1920s, the era that Fitzgerald would christen the Jazz Age. Her essay "Eulogy on the Flapper" offers some insights into her temperament:

How can a girl say again, "I do not want to be respectable because respectable girls are not attractive," and how can she again so wisely arrive at the knowledge that "boys *do* dance most with the girls they kiss most," and that "men *will* marry the girls they could kiss before they had asked papa"? Perceiving these things, the Flapper awoke from her lethargy of sub-deb-ism, bobbed her hair, put on her choicest pair of earrings and a great deal of audacity and rouge, and went into the battle. She flirted because it was fun to flirt and wore a one-piece bathing suit because she had a good figure; she covered her face with powder and paint because she didn't need it and she refused to be bored chiefly because she wasn't boring. She was conscious that the things she did were the things she had always wanted to do.[4]

This dramatic flair and willingness to violate traditional norms of conduct added to Zelda's appeal. It was not long before Fitzgerald fell in love with Zelda, and she reciprocated.

At the same time that Fitzgerald was finding himself in his second great romantic relationship, he was continuing to pursue his writing ambitions. Now he had another reason to seek success as an author, so that he could win the woman of his dreams.

Fitzgerald received his first rejection from Scribners during the month following his first encounter with Zelda. Within six weeks, he had revised *The Romantic Egotist* and resubmitted the manuscript. Perkins was pleased with the revisions but knew that selling the novel to the rest of the editorial staff remained a challenge. To Perkins's disappointment he once again failed to achieve sufficient support to publish the book. Feeling obligated to the author's best interests, he sent the manuscript to two other publishers, simultaneously hoping they would turn it down, for Perkins still hoped to secure Fitzgerald for Scribners. Perkins need not have worried, as they, too, rejected the manuscript.

WAR HEROISM DENIED

Fitzgerald now had three major concerns: his future role in the war, Zelda, and his writing. With the rest of the 67th Infantry, he received orders on October 26, 1918, to report to Camp Mills on Long Island, New York, preparatory to being shipped out to France. Fitzgerald liked to tell the story of marching up the gangplank, receiving news of the armistice, which was announced on November 11, and marching back down. Nothing quite so dramatic actually occurred. In fact, Fitzgerald spent much of his time partying heavily in New York, at one point almost being arrested in a hotel room with a girl, and missing his train when the unit was ordered back to Montgomery in November. He caught up with his unit in Washington, D.C., and back at Camp Sheridan served as aide-de-camp to the camp commander, General A. J. Ryan. As the years passed, Fitzgerald came to regard missing out on an active role in the war as a second major failure (after not graduating from Princeton), a failure magnified when he later became friends with Ernest Hemingway, who had been a genuine war hero in Italy before winning acclaim as a writer. Unlike Hemingway, Fitzgerald would not have personal war experiences to draw upon in his own fiction.

Back at Montgomery, Fitzgerald was able to pursue Zelda at close range, and the romance progressed, although with continuing frustrations for Fitzgerald. He saw Zelda often, called her so many times that for the rest of his life he remembered the Sayres' phone number, and even spent Christmas with her. However, she continued to date others, attending University of Auburn and Georgia Tech proms with Fitzgerald left behind to drown his jealousy and insecurity in drink. Quarrels routinely followed such incidents. Marriage was a common topic between them, but Zelda questioned whether he would earn enough money to make marriage feasible. She had no intention of scrimping and saving while living in a small, cramped apartment to make ends meet. Financial success was essential to Zelda, and Fitzgerald, on his part, accepted these expectations, unable to envision his dream woman settling for a commonplace existence.

EMBARKING UPON A WRITING CAREER

Fitzgerald received his military discharge on February 14, 1919, and knowing that a successful career was essential to winning Zelda, moved to New York to look for work. Only a few weeks earlier, Fitzgerald had received word of the death of Monsignor Fay, who had succumbed to pneumonia on January 10. Responding to the death in a letter to Shane Leslie in late January, Fitzgerald wrote, "This has made me nearly sure that I will become a priest."[5] The statement surely expressed only a passing thought, as Fitzgerald at the time was in Alabama seriously pursuing Zelda and anticipating a writing career. The loss of his longtime mentor and confidant, however, removed a respected and beloved presence. There was no one left who occupied quite the same place in Fitzgerald's life.

Failing to land a newspaper job in New York, he took a position with Barron Collier, an advertising agency, writing slogans for various businesses, such as a jingle for a Muscatine, Iowa, laundry: "We Keep You Clean in Muscatine." This was hardly what Fitzgerald had in mind when he dreamed of success as a novelist, but he continued to write and submit short stories. The result was steady rejections, with Fitzgerald claiming that he had 122 rejection slips hanging on the walls of his one-room apartment.[6]

Despite the sale of "Babes in the Woods" to *Smart Set* in June, the $30 he received for the story purchasing a pair of white flannel trousers,[7] Fitzgerald found his summer of 1919 yielding little progress in love and writing, two concerns that he increasingly understood as linked. In March, he sent Zelda his mother's engagement ring and traveled to Montgomery monthly from April to June attempting to persuade her to a quick marriage. Zelda's faltering commitment to write regular letters enhanced Fitzgerald's uncertainty about her intentions. He later recounted those New York days in an essay entitled "My Lost City":

> As I hovered ghost-like in the Plaza Red Room of a Saturday afternoon, or went to lush and liquid garden parties in the East Sixties or tippled with Princetonians in the Biltmore Bar I was haunted always by my other life—my drab room in the Bronx, my square foot of the subway, my fixation upon the day's letter from Alabama—would it come and what would it say?—my shabby suits, my poverty, and love…. The most hilarious luncheon table or the most moony cabaret—it was all the same; from them I returned eagerly to my home on Claremont Avenue—home because there might be a letter waiting outside the door…. I was a failure—mediocre at advertising work and unable to get started as a writer.[8]

During Fitzgerald's June trip to Montgomery, Zelda broke off the engagement. Fitzgerald returned to New York and attempted to drown his sorrows in a lengthy drunk that lasted until the start of Prohibition on July 1.

Faced with the reality that he was both losing Zelda and making little progress with his fiction, Fitzgerald returned to St. Paul on July 4 and took up residence in a room on the third floor of the house at 599 Summit Avenue to which his parents had recently moved. There he labored steadily at his earlier manuscript, completing a draft (which contained large portions of the novel earlier rejected by Scribners) by the end of July. He called the manuscript *The Education of a Personage*. By the middle of August, he had changed the title to *This Side of Paradise*, retaining "The Romantic Egotist" and "The Education of a Personage" as the titles of book 1 and book 2, respectively. Fearing that the manuscript might be lost in the mail, he asked a friend, Thomas Daniels, to hand deliver it to Max Perkins.

During his stay in St. Paul, he sought recreation generally in a much more subdued manner than in New York, often walking to the corner drugstore with Richard "Tubby" Washington, a friend from St. Paul Academy days, for a Coca-Cola and cigarette. He also enjoyed literary conversations with Donald Ogden Stewart, who would become a well-known humorist, and John Briggs, future headmaster of St. Paul Academy. In addition, despite his claim to be all through with Catholicism,[9] he had many intellectually stimulating discussions with Father Joseph Barron, dean of students at St. Paul Seminary.

Fitzgerald, who had no real source of income, nonetheless rejected an offer to become advertising manager at the St. Paul firm of Griggs Cooper & Company, a wholesaler. After finishing his novel, however, he was persuaded by a friend, Larry Boardman, a supervisor in the Northern Pacific car barn, to work for him while awaiting a response from Scribners.

THIS SIDE OF PARADISE ACCEPTED

The decision regarding his novel came in a letter from Max Perkins dated September 16, 1919, affirming Scribners' desire to publish *This Side of Paradise*. Perkins's letter did not convey the difficulty that he once again had experienced persuading the publisher to commit to Fitzgerald. In fact, Perkins had virtually threatened to resign if Scribners let Fitzgerald get away: "And if we aren't going to publish a talent like this, it is a very serious thing.... If we're going to turn down the likes of Fitzgerald, I will lose all interest in publishing books."[10]

The acceptance letter made no mention of this threat, stating emphatically that "we are all for publishing the book, 'This Side of Paradise.' "[11] The truth is that neither connotation of "all" in the sentence was correct. Not all members of the editorial staff favored publishing the book, nor overall was there great enthusiasm for the project. Perkins made sure that none of the infighting over the manuscript got through to the author to cloud his joy at its acceptance.

And Fitzgerald was ecstatic at the news. Some nineteen years later in the essay "Early Success," he recalled quitting his job and running along streets telling surprised motorists of his literary success.[12]

Although Fitzgerald had not been writing to Zelda, he realized that this success might also translate into a renewal of his engagement with her. Consequently, he responded to Perkins on September 18 pleading for early publication, explaining, "I have so many things dependent on its success—including of course a girl...."[13]

Perkins responded with an explanation of why the usual publishing process needed to go forward for the book to enjoy good sales, and since it was too late for the fall season, Scribners would aim for spring publication.

WINNING ZELDA BACK

While waiting for the spring appearance of his first novel, Fitzgerald made considerable progress regarding winning Zelda back and selling short stories. He wrote Zelda of his news regarding the novel and went to Montgomery to see her in November. Zelda agreed to marriage but delayed the formal announcement of their resumed engagement, a notice in the *Montgomery Journal* not appearing until March 28, 1920, less than a week before their marriage.

Fitzgerald quickly began to place short stories with magazines, helped by his increased confidence in himself as a writer and by the editors' knowledge that the young author was soon to be a published novelist. He began with *The Smart Set*, a relatively small-circulation but highly respected magazine edited by George Jean Nathan and H. L. Mencken, the latter one of the country's most respected literary critics. Over the next few months, he was published four times in *The Smart Set*. Two of the publications were revised *Nassau Literary Magazine* pieces—*The Debutante* and "Benediction" (originally published as "The Ordeal")—and two new stories: "Porcelain and Pink" and "Dalyrimple Goes Wrong."

The Smart Set, though influential, paid no more than $40 per acceptance, so Fitzgerald, looking forward to marriage and not having received an advance for his novel, turned to better-paying magazines. *Scribner's Magazine*, edited by Robert Bridges, accepted "The Cut-Glass Bowl" and "The Four Fists" at $150 each while rejecting several other stories.[14]

Fitzgerald's earnings increased dramatically after signing with the Paul Revere Reynolds literary agency in the fall. Harold Ober, a partner in the firm, became his agent and established a long-lived relationship for Fitzgerald with *The Saturday Evening Post*, which paid $400 for "Head and Shoulders." The *Post*, edited by George Horace Lorimer, would pay as much as $4,000 apiece for Fitzgerald's stories by 1929. By February 1920, he had also sold to the *Post* "Bernice Bobs Her Hair," "The Camel's Back," "The Ice Palace," "Myra Meets His Family," and "The Offshore Pirate."

Despite his success with short stories, Fitzgerald was having difficulty making progress with a second novel. He made several starts on novels variously entitled *The Demon Lover, The Drunkard's Holiday,* and *Darling Heart* but quickly abandoned them. The short stories, though, came easily and produced quick money. Fitzgerald's need for money remained a problem throughout his life, the result of spending beyond his means even when he was earning a substantial income, and later because of financial expenses associated with Zelda's illness. The answer often would be a combination of borrowing, especially from Ober, and requesting advances on future novels through Perkins, while dashing off another story. Although Fitzgerald's best stories are literary classics, he consistently drew a distinction between them and his novels, often shortchanging the quality of his stories. Short stories in his view were what he did to earn money; novels were what he did as a literary artist, although he also expected his novels to be commercial successes. Money from the short stories made it possible to devote time to the

NOTES

1. A. Scott Berg, *Max Perkins: Editor of Genius* (1978; New York: Pocket oks, 1979), 14.

2. *Correspondence of F. Scott Fitzgerald*, ed. Matthew J. Bruccoli and Margaret Duggan (New York: Random House, 1980), 31–32.

3. *The Short Stories of F. Scott Fitzgerald*, ed. Matthew J. Bruccoli (1989; w York: Simon and Schuster, 1995), 51.

4. Zelda Fitzgerald, *The Collected Writings*, ed. Matthew J. Bruccoli (1991; w York: Collier Books, 1992), 391.

5. *The Letters of F. Scott Fitzgerald*, ed. Andrew Turnbull (1963; New York: ll, 1965), 375.

6. Arthur Mizener, *The Far Side of Paradise: A Biography of F. Scott Fitzgerald*, . ed. (Boston: Houghton Mifflin, 1965), 86.

7. F. Scott Fitzgerald, "Auction—Model 1934," in *The Crack-Up*, . Edmund Wilson (1945; New York: New Directions, 1956), 59.

8. *The Crack-Up*, 25–26. Matthew J. Bruccoli has pointed out in *Some Sort Epic Grandeur: The Life of F. Scott Fitzgerald*, 2nd rev. ed. (Columbia: University South Carolina Press, 2002) that Fitzgerald's reference to having lived in the onx is most likely incorrect, and that he actually lived in Manhattan (96).

9. In his *Ledger*, on the page for the year beginning with his twenty-first thday (1917–18), Fitzgerald writes, "A year of enormous importance. Work, and lda. Last year as a Catholic." See *F. Scott Fitzgerald's Ledger: A Facsimile*, edited Matthew J. Bruccoli (Washington, DC: NCR/Microcard Editions, 1972), 172. zgerald began keeping the ledger as he embarked upon a professional writing eer, around 1919–20 (adding information pertaining to his earlier life), and ntinued it to 1937. It includes records of publications and earnings, as well as outline of his life.

10. Berg, *Max Perkins*, 18.

11. *Dear Scott/Dear Max: The Fitzgerald-Perkins Correspondence*, ed. John Kuehl d Jackson R. Bryer (New York: Scribners, 1971), 21.

12. *The Crack-Up*, 86.

13. *Dear Scott/Dear Max*, 21.

14. I am indebted to appendix 2 of Bruccoli's *Some Sort of Epic Grandeur*, ecially pp. 524–43, for information on Fitzgerald's earnings.

15. For a discussion of the influence of Fitzgerald's Catholicism on him, see n M. Allen, *Candles and Carnival Lights: The Catholic Sensibility of F. Scott zgerald* (New York: New York University Press, 1978).

16. Sally Cline, *Zelda Fitzgerald: Her Voice in Paradise* (New York: Arcade blishing, 2002), 74–76.

novels, but his lifestyle increasingly militated against novels, bc
he consistently needed money and because his health, which d
badly during the 1930s, made prolonged concentration and eff(

Fitzgerald went to New Orleans in January 1920 for inspira
be closer to Zelda but did not find the setting conducive to
February, he moved to New York City and was there when O|
movie rights for "Head and Shoulders" to Metro Films for $2,5
at the age of twenty-three that he had embarked upon a gold(
would stretch steadily into the future, he celebrated the sale \
liquor and extravagant spending. He deliberately arranged l
they would hang from his pockets and tipped lavishly.

Near the end of February, Fitzgerald moved to Princeton
the Cottage Club and await the publication of *This Side of*
no doubt felt at least partly vindicated celebrating his publi{
where he had endured so many earlier disappointments.

MARRIAGE

The novel appeared on March 26, 1920, and on April 3 I
Zelda were married in the rectory of St. Patrick's Cathedral
The setting was something of a compromise, a Catholic catl
the church portion itself, and no wedding mass. Fitzgerald
a practicing Catholic, although his Catholicism would con
throughout his life in his fiction.[15] The Sayres were Episcopa
the difference in religion mattered less to them than their <
Fitzgerald's financial stability. Ludlow Fowler, a Princeton fi
man; Rosalind Smith, one of Zelda's three sisters, was matror
other two sisters, Marjorie and Clothilde, also planned to at
a nervous Scott insisted that the ceremony occur even be
and her husband, John Palmer, were scheduled to arrive.
parents attended; nor did Zelda's brother, Anthony.

After the wedding, the couple, minus any sort of recept
dinner, departed for their honeymoon at the Biltmore Ho
three sisters upset at the sparse event and its rushed plan/
bones event—no music, photographers, flowers, celebratory
(except for the best man)—as Zelda's biographer Sally C|
tured, must have left Zelda disappointed and feeling vastl
the princess she had been treated as during her youth in N
was an inauspicious beginning for a marriage that would ea
make society columns but suffer enormous, tragic difficult

Chapter 4

EARLY SUCCESS: *THIS SIDE OF PARADISE* AND THE JAZZ AGE (1920–1922)

THE JAZZ AGE

The decade of the 1920s was variously known as the Roaring Twenties and the Jazz Age, the latter term generally credited to F. Scott Fitzgerald. It was a time seemingly dominated by its "flaming youth," the expression adopted from the title of a 1923 novel by Samuel Hopkins Adams and popularized further by the film version starring Colleen Moore.[1] Young women known as flappers wore short skirts, bobbed their hair, danced the Charleston, and smoked in public. The Eighteenth Amendment to the U.S. Constitution, effective in January 1920, outlawed the manufacture, sale, transportation, and importation (as well as exporting) of intoxicating liquors and was implemented in July following a Supreme Court decision upholding the amendment's legality. Nonetheless, there was a boom in illegal drinking, including among the young, who often found even more excitement in seeking the forbidden. Speakeasies proliferated in cities and towns, while individuals throughout the country concocted their own versions of "bathtub gin."

Manufacturing expanded rapidly during the decade, helped by the assembly line, increased use of electricity, and new labor-saving machinery. Among the items pouring off the assembly lines were automobiles, which tripled in number, from some nine million at the beginning of the decade to about twenty-seven million by the end. Young men and women coming of age during the decade were the first generation to have ready access to automobiles, which offered greater freedom of action away from the censoring eyes of their parents. More liberal sexual mores went hand-in-hand with other aspects of the changing lifestyle. Never had the young wielded so much influence and claimed so much attention in American society.[2]

The first radio station was established in 1920, KDKA in Pittsburgh, and among other attractions, listeners could follow the exploits of such sports heroes as baseball slugger Babe Ruth, football great Red Grange, boxing champion Jack Dempsey, golfer Bobby Jones, and football coach Knute Rockne, who was transforming the University of Notre Dame football team into a perennial powerhouse. The greatest hero of them all, though, was the young aviator Charles Lindbergh, who in 1927 became the first person to make a solo transatlantic flight.

If women were treading on male ground with short haircuts and public drinking and smoking, they also stepped more fully into the role of U.S. citizens as a result of the Nineteenth Amendment to the Constitution. Ratified in August 1920, it declared, "The right of citizens of the United States to vote shall not be denied or abridged by the United States or by any State on account of sex." From then on, politicians would have to court the women's vote as well as the men's.

The 1920s thus marked a radical change in American society, fueled by growth in manufacturing and merchandising, the expansion of industry to the West and South, increased wages and profits, the growing practice of buying on credit, and, perhaps most importantly—and most dangerously—a sky-high bull market. Those who had the money to invest jumped into the market with both feet, investing their futures in a belief, as Fitzgerald wrote, that "life was like the race in *Alice in Wonderland*, there was a prize for every one."[3]

This was the world, heady, vibrant, awash in optimism, into which the young author and his bride stepped. F. Scott Fitzgerald would soon be perceived as both the embodiment and the spokesperson of his generation. At the same time, his life would follow a path parallel to that of the era. The decade began on a high note for him and for millions of Americans, although not, of course, for everyone. Farmers, mill workers, miners, and many others on the whole were left behind by the decade's prosperity. By the end of the decade, the Roaring Twenties disintegrated in the stock market crash of 1929 that ushered in what became known as the Great Depression. Fitzgerald's life also collapsed about him by the end of the 1920s, the glittering promise of those early years dimmed amid alcoholism, financial troubles, and Zelda's mental illness. As it is possible in retrospect to chart various economic factors throughout the 1920s that helped precipitate Black Tuesday, October 29, 1929, the day of the great Wall Street collapse—for example, unrealistically high stock prices, technological lay-offs caused by industrial innovations, extensive buying on credit, and a warning recession marked by sharp drops in home construction and automobile sales—so too is it possible to see in the years of Fitzgerald's success the causes of his collapse, or, as he would call it, his "crack-up."[4]

THIS SIDE OF PARADISE

But in 1920, the world seemed made for Scott and Zelda Fitzgerald. First, there were the publishing successes. *This Side of Paradise,* released on March 26, 1920, sold well and received generally positive reviews. Although not a top-ten seller, it went through twelve printings by the end of 1921, selling close to 50,000 copies.

Many of the major characters were based on real individuals, which helped them come alive on the page. Amory Blaine, the protagonist, is heavily autobiographical, with much of the novel devoted to his years at Princeton. His love interests, Isabelle and Rosalind, reflect Fitzgerald's own two great loves, Ginevra King and Zelda. Monsignor Darcy is modeled closely on Scott's mentor and confidant, Father Fay. A number of Princeton friends of the author appear in the novel, including John Peale Bishop as the poetic Thomas Park D'Invilliers and Henry Strater, future painter but better known on campus as a leader of the anti-club movement, as Burne Holiday.

The novel proved popular for several reasons. Readers saw it as a reflection of the radical change occurring in society with the rise of a daring and tradition-defying youth culture. The setting and concerns of the characters made the novel a different type of college novel, one representing, for readers, the realities of campus life in postwar America. The novel also presented the new woman in her sexually liberated mode, even if by later standards that sexual liberation seems fairly limited. Sexual activity within the novel remains largely at the level of kissing. Although referred to as petting, it is what a later generation would call necking. Despite the greater sexual frankness, the novel retains a definite moral tone, even a fairly conservative one. When Amory finds himself in an apartment with a friend and two women, his temptation is obliterated by a vision of a devil-like man wearing "no shoes, but, instead, a sort of half moccasin, pointed, though, like the shoes they wore in the fourteenth century, and with the little ends curling up." As the divan on which the man sits comes "alive like heat waves over asphalt, like wriggling worms," Amory flees.[5]

The novel is a bildungsroman, a coming-of-age story, chronicling a progression noted in the titles of the two major sections of the book from a young man who is a "romantic egotist" (until the end of his college years) through the process known as "the education of a personage," which occurs after his return from war. Amory relies on Monsignor Darcy to explain the change from being a mere personality to a personage: "Personality is a physical matter almost entirely; it lowers the people it acts on—I've seen it vanish in a long sickness. But while a personality is active, it overrides 'the next thing.' Now a personage, on the other hand, gathers. He is never thought of apart from what he's done."[6]

The distinction between personality and personage, though, is never defined precisely, and ultimately what Amory learns seems somewhat unsatisfactory and confused. Returning to Princeton at the end of the novel in a world in which the new generation has found "all Gods dead, all wars fought, all faiths in man shaken," Amory realizes a trade-off. The "waters of disillusion" have stripped him of old beliefs in religion and the ability to share in "the fear of poverty and the worship of success," yet the stripping has "left a deposit on his soul, responsibility and a love of life...." Yet, "it's all a poor substitute at best," he thinks. Finally, he stretches his arms outward toward the sky: "'I know myself,' he cried, 'but that is all.'"[7] That, of course, can be a great deal. It certainly is a vital step toward wisdom.

Fitzgerald presents a brief Interlude between the two sections of the novel, covering the period May 1917 to February 1919. Amory has been to war, but given Fitzgerald's lack of first-hand knowledge of the conflict, he wisely does not attempt a detailed accounting.

The novel appealed also because of what seemed its radical innovation in narrative approach. The novel includes poems and short plays along with the prose. Later readers were likely to see Fitzgerald incorporating his life and earlier writings into the story in as many ways as he could, with some disjointedness resulting from the mix. There also is some literary pretentiousness in the novel, a quality Zelda pointed out in a part playful, part serious review of the later *Beautiful and Damned*. Her comment applies as well to *This Side of Paradise*: "The other things that I didn't like in the book—I mean the unimportant things—were the literary references and the attempt to convey a profound air of erudition."[8] A later critic tabulated the novel's literary references, identifying sixty-four titles and ninety-eight writers.[9] On the other hand, bright, literary-minded college students were likely then, as they are today, to engage in serious literary discussions, especially those students on their way to becoming renowned writers.

Within a few weeks of the novel's publication, Fitzgerald wrote a self-interview that includes a remarkably prescient statement: "The wise writer, I think, writes for the youth of his own generation, the critic of the next and the schoolmasters of ever afterward."[10] Certainly Fitzgerald struck a resounding chord with his own generation, and the critical world, shortly after his death in 1940, initiated a great flowering of scholarly and popular interest in Fitzgerald. The omnipresence of his fiction, especially *The Great Gatsby* and a number of his short stories, in high school and college curricula today testifies to the accuracy of the final element in his assertion.

This Side of Paradise stamped its author as the spokesperson for a generation in revolt against the traditions of the past, and subsequent books reinforced Fitzgerald's special place within the Jazz Age. The collection of short stories that followed the novel in 1920 further cemented the association of author and era. Scribners, consistent with its practice of capitalizing on the appearance of a novel by bringing out a collection of stories by the same author, released *Flappers and Philosophers* in September. The volume included eight stories, the most important of which were "Bernice Bobs Her Hair" and "The Ice Palace." Collections of short stories almost never prove as popular as novels, but *Flappers and Philosophers* did well, selling more than 15,000 copies in little over a year.

THE BEAUTIFUL AND DAMNED

Fitzgerald followed these first books in short order with a second novel, *The Beautiful and Damned*, about the disintegration of a young couple, Anthony and Gloria Patch. Early in the novel, Anthony is waiting to inherit a fortune from his grandfather. Ultimately, the inheritance arrives, but in the meantime Anthony has undergone, helped along by alcohol, steady erosion of his character; and Gloria, a partner in her husband's self-destructive lifestyle, loses her beauty. Another character in the novel, Dick Caramel, is a writer who seems to sell out to commercial success. It is easy, in light of later personal developments, to read the novel as a self-cautionary account of what might befall the author himself and his wife.

The Beautiful and Damned was serialized in *Metropolitan* magazine from September 1921 to March 1922, the month in which it was published by Scribners. *The Beautiful and Damned* received fewer positive reviews than the earlier novel even though it demonstrates a growing ability on the part of the author to construct a coherent narrative. Some of the negative reaction was because reviewers expected a novel more in line with the earlier one in subject and style. It also sold less well, although it was by no means a commercial failure. The novel went through three printings and about 50,000 copies in 1922. Among the novels that outsold *The Beautiful and Damned* was Robert Keable's *Simon Called Peter*, an account of an army chaplain and his passions. Fitzgerald considered the novel one of "the really immoral books"[11] and resented a book he considered artistically and morally inferior to his own novel proving more popular than his. Revenge came in *The Great Gatsby*, where Keable's novel reappears in the New York apartment that Tom Buchanan uses for his love trysts with Myrtle Wilson. Nick Carraway finds it lying on a table with copies of *Town Tattle* and some Broadway scandal magazines as examples of bad taste and a fondness for the prurient.[12]

Whereas Fitzgerald had made extensive use of his own life in *This Side of Paradise*, with the second novel he began to draw upon experiences that constituted joint property with Zelda. In her review of the new novel, Zelda noted:

> It seems to me on one page I recognized a portion of an old diary of mine which mysteriously disappeared shortly after my marriage, and also scraps of letters which, though considerably edited, sound to me vaguely familiar. In fact, Mr. Fitzgerald—I believe that is how he spells his name—seems to believe that plagiarism begins at home.[13]

The practice of appropriating joint experiences would become a source of serious contention in later years, especially when Zelda drew upon their life together for her novel *Save Me the Waltz* in 1932, at a time Fitzgerald was struggling to complete *Tender Is the Night*. By virtue of his more established authorial career, Fitzgerald viewed himself as proper owner of the writing rights to their marriage and had been using Zelda and their experiences together in his fiction since meeting her.

Again Scribners followed the novel with a collection of short stories, *Tales of the Jazz Age*, the title highlighting the author's special relationship to the times. The finest stories in the volume are "May Day" and "The Diamond as Big as the Ritz," although the two stories, now recognized as among Fitzgerald's best, did not receive much serious attention at the time.

Tales of the Jazz Age, its dust jacket adorned with Jazz Age cartoon characters drawn by the famous cartoonist John Held, Jr., sold well, with three printings during 1922.[14] Not long removed from his days of compiling an unbroken chain of rejections, Fitzgerald now had published four books within two and one-half years, and he was recognized as one of the most popular and promising young authors in America, appearing in *Who's Who in America* for the first time in 1921.

REPRESENTATIVES OF AN ERA

Along with his growing renown as a writer, Fitzgerald and Zelda were becoming famous as one of America's most dazzling and exciting couples. There was no shortage of newspaper accounts of Scott and Zelda as they consistently made good copy, exhibiting high spirits and rejecting traditional behavior with such antics as riding on the roof of a taxi or jumping fully clothed into a fountain.[15] Fitzgerald liked being the life of the party, and to that end he sometimes entertained other guests by performing a song entitled "Dog! Dog! Dog!" that he and Edmund Wilson had composed. Always looking for material for his fiction, even when it involved using his own failings, Fitzgerald has Joel Coles make a fool of himself performing a comedy routine called "Building It Up" at a party in the story "Crazy Sunday," published in 1932.

Even from the first, though, Fitzgerald and Zelda's antics tended to cross the line from a spirited good time to exhibitionism, and their drinking increasingly became obtrusive. Fitzgerald especially had great difficulty holding his liquor and tended when drinking to lose self-control quickly. After their marriage on April 3, 1920, the couple had moved into the Biltmore Hotel in New York. Within the month, they were asked to leave because their partying was bothering other guests. They moved to the Commodore Hotel and celebrated the arrival by spinning around repeatedly in the revolving door.

Later in the month, Fitzgerald took Zelda to Princeton, where he pretended she was his mistress and incurred a black eye at a party. When he returned to Princeton a few days later with Edmund Wilson and John Peale Bishop for a *Nassau Lit* banquet, he incurred the wrath of Cottage Club members for dressing like Apollo with a wreath and lyre and was suspended from club membership.

In May, the Fitzgeralds purchased a Marmon touring car and moved to Westport, Connecticut, where they rented a house. They spent the summer there except for a trip to Montgomery to visit Zelda's family, a visit that Judge and Mrs. Sayre reciprocated in August. The stay in Westport was a time of little work and much partying and heavy drinking. Zelda flirted regularly, her behavior ranging from kissing men at parties to asking Townsend Martin to give her a bath. George Jean Nathan took the flirting seriously enough that Fitzgerald ended their friendship with him. Zelda spent lavishly on clothes and jewelry while refusing to do even basic housekeeping. Fitzgerald's growing unhappiness with their stay in Connecticut is reflected in "The Diamond as Big as the Ritz" as he places in Westport the insane asylum to which a group of former workers on the Washington chateau, the luxurious Washington home, are confined.

The Fitzgeralds returned to New York in October, renting an apartment. By February of 1921, Zelda discovered that she was pregnant. Following another visit to Montgomery, they set sail on May 3 to Europe on the *Aquitania*, hoping to enjoy their first European trip before Zelda became too uncomfortable to travel well. They toured England, France, and Italy, but with a few exceptions—visiting Shane Leslie in London and seeing the house in Rome where Keats died, for example—they did not enjoy the experience. Sightseeing proved boring, perhaps because it was too passive of a pastime for the young couple accustomed to being the center of attention. In addition, they resented European culture. Fitzgerald wrote Edmund Wilson from London in May expressing his disdain for Europe in tones heavy with racist and nationalistic superiority, along with self-awareness of his bias:

> God damn the continent of Europe. It is of merely antiquarian interest.... The negroid streak creeps northward to defile the Nordic race.... France made me sick. Its silly pose as the thing the world has to save. I think it's a shame that England and America didn't let Germany conquer Europe.... My reactions were all philistine, antisocialistic, provincial and racially snobbish. I believe at last in the white man's burden. We are as far above the modern Frenchman as he is above the Negro.[16]

Cutting short their European tour, the Fitzgeralds returned to the United States in July.

After another Montgomery trip, the couple, wanting to escape the Southern heat during Zelda's final stages of pregnancy, moved to the St. Paul area, taking a house at Dellwood on White Bear Lake. This also offered an opportunity for Zelda to meet Fitzgerald's parents, who had not attended their son's wedding.

In St. Paul, Fitzgerald established a friendship with Thomas Boyd, literary editor of the *St. Paul Daily News*, who interviewed the favorite-son author for the paper. Beginning a practice of encouraging other authors and especially trying to link them up with his own publisher, Fitzgerald recommended both Boyd and his wife, Peggy, who wrote as Woodward Boyd, to Scribners. The firm published both novelists, beginning with Peggy Boyd's *The Love Legend* in 1922. Thomas Boyd's first novel, *Through the Wheat*, appeared in 1923. His autobiographical novel of World War I marines remains an important account of the war from a soldier's perspective.[17] The generosity that Fitzgerald demonstrated toward the Boyds and other young writers, including Ernest Hemingway a few years later, would remain an abiding characteristic of the author. As Hemingway wrote years later in A Moveable Feast, he "had no more loyal friend than Scott when he was sober."[18]

SCOTTIE, THEIR DAUGHTER

Evicted from their White Bear Lake house by the owner, who blamed them for some damage to the house, Fitzgerald and Zelda transferred to an apartment hotel called the Commodore in his parents' Summit Avenue neighborhood of St. Paul to await their child's birth. Frances Scott "Scottie" Fitzgerald was born on October 26, 1921, at the Miller Hospital in St. Paul. Still partly under the anesthesia, Zelda offered an unusual wish for her daughter, quoted by Fitzgerald in his Ledger: "I hope its [sic] beautiful and a fool—a beautiful little fool."[19] The statement would reappear in The Great Gatsby as Daisy's wish for her daughter, Pammy: "I woke up out of the ether with an utterly abandoned feeling and asked the nurse right away if it was a boy or a girl. She told me it was a girl, and so I turned my head away and wept. 'All right,' I said, 'I'm glad it's a girl. And I hope she'll be a fool—that's the best thing a girl can be in this world, a beautiful little fool.' "[20]

The daughter was named Scottie on her birth certificate and called that throughout her life. Despite Fitzgerald's earlier disavowal of Catholicism, he had Scottie baptized at the Convent of the Visitation, home to the order of nuns that his Grandfather McQuillan had helped bring to St. Paul and who had educated both Fitzgerald's mother and sister.

The following month, the enlarged family rented a house on Goodrich Avenue, also in the Summit Avenue area, for the winter. Zelda hated the cold weather, a characteristic shared with Sally Carrol Happer in "The Ice Palace," although the story antedated the Fitzgeralds' St. Paul winter.

The Fitzgeralds went to New York for the March 1922 publication of The Beautiful and Damned. While there, Zelda, pregnant again, had an abortion to avoid having two children so close together.[21] Returning to the St. Paul area for the summer, the Fitzgeralds stayed at the White Bear Yacht Club in Dellwood. Fitzgerald worked on a play, The Vegetable, prepared Tales of the Jazz Age for publication, and wrote a story called "The Curious Case of Benjamin Button" about a man who undergoes a reverse chronology, from old age to infancy. He also finished "Winter Dreams," the first of the stories often referred to as the Gatsby cluster stories. "Winter Dreams" introduces in Dexter Green a young man who acquires wealth as a means of winning the desirable but ultimately unwinnable girl of his dreams, Judy Jones. The story thus anticipates in theme and characterization the relationship between Gatsby and Daisy Buchanan in *The Great Gatsby*.

The summer of 1922 also included a number of parties, the rambunctious nature of which led to the Fitzgeralds being forced to leave the Yacht Club, expulsions from residences, usually because of their high living, having by now become a way of life. They wanted, however, to return to New York anyway as Fitzgerald looked forward to seeing his play produced on Broadway, an expectation that would never materialize. They therefore left Scottie temporarily in St. Paul and went to New York in search of a place to rent.

As the Fitzgeralds prepared to move to New York, the Jazz Age was in full swing, and New York was the place to be for those who reveled in the period's possibilities. In the fall of 1922, Scott and Zelda Fitzgerald seemed on top of the world. They were young, beautiful, and famous. Scott had become a successful author with four books published and more surely on the way, earning him both fame and at least moderate fortune. The couple had already journeyed to Europe, albeit without a great deal of enjoyment, and they had a child that they both loved. Everything appeared to be going their way, and the prevailing mood of both their life together and of society was one of continuing optimism. Unfortunately, neither the Fitzgeralds nor the broader society understood the problems that already were undermining their future prosperity and health.

NOTES

1. Adams (1871–1958), best known as a muckraking reporter for *McClure's Magazine* and *Collier's Weekly*, a series of articles on fraudulent medicine claims for the latter helping lead to passage of the Pure Food and Drug Act in 1906, published *Flaming Youth* under the pseudonym Warner Fabian. In his essay "Echoes of the Jazz Age," available in *The Crack-Up*, ed. Edmund Wilson (1945; New York: New Directions, 1956), Fitzgerald incorrectly assigns Clara Bow to the 1923 film version of *Flaming Youth* instead of Colleen Moore (17).

2. Among many excellent books on the 1920s, an especially detailed and comprehensive overview occurs in Geoffrey Perrett's *America in the Twenties: A History* (1982; New York: Simon and Schuster, 1983).

3. "Echoes of the Jazz Age," in *The Crack-Up*, 21.

4. Perrett gives considerable attention to economic factors leading to the stock market crash and the Great Depression, especially in part 3, "Belshazzar's Feast" (301–90).

5. F. Scott Fitzgerald, *This Side of Paradise* (1920; New York: Scribners, 2003), 109.

6. Ibid., 101.

7. Ibid., 260.

8. "Friend Husband's Latest," in *Zelda Fitzgerald: The Collected Writings*, ed. Matthew J. Bruccoli (1991; New York: Collier Books, 1992), 388–89.

9. Dorothy B. Good, "'Romance and a Reading List': The Literary References in *This Side of Paradise*," *Fitzgerald/Hemingway Annual* (1976): 35–64.

10. "Self-Interview: An Interview with F. Scott Fitzgerald," in *F. Scott Fitzgerald in His Own Time: A Miscellany*, ed. Matthew J. Bruccoli and Jackson R. Bryer (1971; New York: Popular Library, 1976), 162.

11. *The Letters of F. Scott Fitzgerald*, ed. Andrew Turnbull (1963; New York: Dell, 1965), 476.

12. F. Scott Fitzgerald, *The Great Gatsby*, preface and notes by Matthew J. Bruccoli (1925; New York: Collier Books, 1992), 33.

13. "Friend Husband's Latest," 388.

14. For Held's life and reproductions of some of his art, see Shelley Armitage, *John Held, Jr.: Illustrator of the Jazz Age* (Syracuse, NY: Syracuse University Press, 1987).

15. *The Romantic Egoists*, ed. Matthew J. Bruccoli and Scottie Fitzgerald Smith (New York: Scribners, 1974), includes many reproductions of newspaper clippings along with much other visual material.

16. *The Letters of F. Scott Fitzgerald*, 326.

17. A recent paperback edition of *Through the Wheat: A Novel of the World War I Marines*, with a useful biographical introduction by Edwin Howard Simmons, is available (Lincoln: University of Nebraska Press, 2000).

18. Ernest Hemingway, *A Moveable Feast* (1964; New York: Collier Books, 1987), 184.

19. *F. Scott Fitzgerald's Ledger: A Facsimile*, edited by Matthew J. Bruccoli (Washington, DC: NCR/Microcard Editions, 1972), 176.

20. *The Great Gatsby*, 21.

21. There is a possibility that Zelda had as many as three abortions. See Sara Mayfield, *Exiles from Paradise: Zelda and Scott Fitzgerald* (New York: Delacorte, 1971), 79–80, 109, 116. Mayfield grew up in Alabama near Zelda and remained a lifelong friend of hers.

Chapter 5

LONG ISLAND AND
THE GREAT GATSBY:
"WHAT A GROTESQUE THING
A ROSE IS" (1922–1925)

GREAT NECK, LONG ISLAND

The Fitzgeralds went house hunting in September 1922, settling on a house at 6 Gateway Drive in Great Neck, Long Island, for $300 per month. The house stood on the north shore of Long Island, approximately fifteen miles from New York City.

Great Neck, which would become the setting for Fitzgerald's next and finest novel, *The Great Gatsby,* provided Fitzgerald with famous and wealthy neighbors, luxuriant estates, and much raw material for the novel. Ed Wynn and Eddie Cantor, both popular comedic actors, and songwriter Gene Buck lived nearby. So did writer and former sports journalist Ring Lardner, best known for his collection of baseball stories *You Know Me Al,* who became a close friend of both Scott and Zelda. An alcoholic, Lardner was a drinking partner of Scott, by then well on his own way to alcoholism. Lardner also was fond of Zelda and addressed humorous poems to her. Fitzgerald, always anxious to assist writer friends, encouraged Lardner to take his short stories more seriously and brought him and Max Perkins together. Scribners ultimately would publish seven of Lardner's books, starting with a collection of short fiction, *How to Write Short Stories,* in 1924. An eighth volume, edited by Gilbert Seldes at Fitzgerald's request and consisting of nonfiction pieces, appeared in 1934 after Lardner's death.

Other acquaintances on Long Island had a more direct effect on Fitzgerald's novel. He acknowledged Herbert Bayard Swope, executive editor of the *New York World* and a giver of lavish parties, as a source for chapter 3, which includes the brilliantly described party Gatsby throws and to which he invites the novel's narrator and Gatsby's next-door neighbor, Nick Carraway.[1]

Edward M. Fuller, who also had an estate at Great Neck and was president of a New York brokerage firm, had burst upon the Wall Street scene virtually from nowhere. He quickly began to travel in high-society circles and regularly flew his own plane. During the Fitzgeralds' stay at Great Neck, Fuller was in the news as one of the defendants in the Fuller-McGee case, accused with the vice president of his firm, William F. McGee, of gambling with their customers' money. It required four trials, all during Fitzgerald's time in Great Neck, finally to convict Fuller. Among those implicated, though not convicted, by Fuller's testimony was Charles Stoneham, owner of the New York Giants baseball team, who, according to Fuller, had been a silent partner in Fuller's firm. Fitzgerald closely studied accounts of the Fuller case and drew heavily on him—his mysterious background, his involvement in criminal stock transactions, even Fuller's fondness for planes—in drawing the character of Gatsby. Stoneham appears to have gone into the creation of Gatsby's mentor, Dan Cody.[2]

Fuller was reputed to be an associate of Arnold Rothstein, usually identified as the man behind fixing the 1919 World Series. In the novel, Gatsby introduces Nick to Meyer Wolfshiem, "the man who fixed the World's Series back in 1919," during a trip into New York.[3] So clear is it to Nick that Wolfshiem and Gatsby had a long relationship that at Gatsby's death Nick tries to persuade him to attend the funeral, even going into the city to make a personal plea. According to Rothstein's biographer, David Pietrusza, Fitzgerald apparently met the real-life model for Wolfshiem only once and had little personal familiarity with the gambler.[4]

Another Long Island acquaintance who provided inspiration for Gatsby was Max Gerlach. Like Gatsby a shadowy figure who may have been involved in illegal schemes, Gerlach is the source for Gatsby's favorite phrase "old sport," which so infuriated Tom Buchanan. Gerlach inscribed a newspaper photo of Scott and Zelda to the couple with the query, "How are you and the family old Sport?"[5]

The Great Neck years, however, saw limited progress on the novel as other matters occupied Fitzgerald's time, including a film contract, short stories (which consistently provided the quick money Fitzgerald always seemed to need), and his play, *The Vegetable*. He landed a film contract with Famous Players in March 1923 for *This Side of Paradise*. The agreement called for Fitzgerald to write a treatment for the film; the sale of film rights brought in $10,000, but the film was not produced. Fitzgerald also wrote an original story for the film *Grit* and titles for the film version of Edith Wharton's *Glimpses of the Moon,* projects that helped boost his earnings from the movies for 1923 to $13,500.[6]

THE VEGETABLE AND SHORT STORIES

Failing to secure production of his play, Fitzgerald published *The Vegetable or from President to Postman* in April 1923. The play is a political satire about a postman who, nagged by his wife to aspire to something more than a mere postman, becomes president of the United States in an alcohol-induced dream. The point behind the title is that anyone who lacks great ambition is nothing more than a vegetable. However, President Jerry Frost makes such a mess of things in his high position that, awakening, he finally finds contentment in being a mere postman.

Fitzgerald, though, continued to seek a producer, succeeding later that year when Sam H. Harris agreed to take the play on. *The Vegetable* opened in November at Nixon's Apollo Theatre in Atlantic City, New Jersey, but its one-week run was a great disappointment. Fitzgerald did some rewriting, but after the play again failed in Stamford, Connecticut, production efforts ceased. Despite Fitzgerald's extensive early experiences with drama in St. Paul and at Princeton, his career as a playwright was over.

With short stories, Fitzgerald was much more successful. He entered into an agreement with the Hearst Magazine Group in 1923 to provide six stories for $1,500 each. The stories included "Dice, Brassknuckles & Guitar," published in *Hearst's International.* The story tells of a Southerner, Jim Powell, who comes north to make his way. He becomes friends with Amanthis, a young woman of high social status, who, commiserating with Jim when he is slighted by other members of her social class, tells him, "'You're better than all of them put together, Jim." The sentence closely anticipates Nick's judgment on Gatsby the last time that he sees him: "'They're a rotten crowd,' I shouted, across the lawn. 'You're worth the whole damn bunch put together.'"[7]

Aspiring to even higher fees for his stories, Fitzgerald returned to *The Saturday Evening Post* in 1924, increasing his per-story pay to $1,750, a figure that would rise to $4,000 by 1929. Fitzgerald wrote a total of ten stories within the first three months of the year, trying, as always, to earn enough money from his short fiction to set aside time for work on his novels. Among his most important stories of 1924 were "The Sensible Thing," another testing of the Gatsby theme, and "Absolution," although neither story appeared in the *Post.* "The Sensible Thing," published in *Liberty,* is about a young impoverished man who loses a wealthy Southern girl because of his poverty. When he returns, having made his fortune, he realizes that what had existed between them before has been lost and that the past cannot be reclaimed, a lesson that Gatsby emphatically denies in the later novel. "Absolution" was, at one time and in some form, part of the Gatsby manuscript before Fitzgerald split it off into a separate story that he placed in *The American Mercury*. Although the details of young Rudolph Miller's life are very different from the childhood of James Gatz (the birth name of Jay Gatsby), Rudolph shares with the older character unhappiness with an impoverished early state and a powerful capacity for dreaming. Even the Coney Island scene on the dust jacket of the novel parallels the advice given Rudolph by Father Schwartz: "'Well, go and see an amusement park.... But don't get up close,' he warned Rudolph, 'because if you do you'll only feel the heat and the sweat and the life.'"[8]

Fitzgerald also wrote several articles on Jazz Age mores while at Great Neck ("Why Blame It on the Poor Kiss If the Girl Veteran of Many Petting Parties Is Prone to Affairs After Marriage?" "Does a Moment of Revolt Come Sometime to Every Married Man?" "What Kind of Husbands Do 'Jimmies' Make?" "Wait Till You Have Children of Your Own"), plus, for *The Saturday Evening Post,* an article tellingly entitled "How to Live on $36,000 a Year." That figure was higher than his income for 1923—close to $29,000. However, as high as his actual income was for the times, he found that he and Zelda could not live on it. One answer for Fitzgerald was to find a place where he could live more economically and work more effectively on his novel, although the truth of his lifestyle was that he would not practice even a modicum of frugality, so everyplace was expensive for him.

THE RIVIERA

Thus, in April 1924, Scott, Zelda, and Scottie sailed for Europe, destination the Riviera. They rented the Villa Marie in Valescure, about a mile and a half north of St. Raphaël. However, with rent, salaries for a nanny, cook, and maid, purchasing a Renault, and extensive spending at area restaurants and other night spots, the money went about as rapidly as it did anywhere else.

Then came one of the turning points in Scott and Zelda's marriage. A French aviator named Edouard Jozan, who would later command a flotilla at Dunkirk during World War II and rise to vice admiral of the French navy in the 1950s, became infatuated with Zelda. As young American fliers had done back in Montgomery, Jozan, a year and two days older than Zelda, buzzed her home, the Villa Marie, in his plane. More seriously, Jozan and Zelda's relationship raised doubts in Fitzgerald regarding whether he could trust his wife. As he wrote in his notebooks, "That

September 1924, I knew something had happened that could never be repaired."[9] Jozan was transferred to Indochina in October, ending what he later claimed was a mere flirtation. That may have been the officer and gentleman refusing to kiss and tell. Or it may indeed have been true that the relationship did not progress to the level of an affair.

The latter is probably more likely. Gerald Murphy, who with his wife, Sara, became friends with the Fitzgeralds that summer, believed that not much came of the relationship, although Zelda's biographer Nancy Milford recounts Scott telling a relative that Zelda had told him in July that she loved Jozan and asked for a divorce, only to back down when Scott insisted on a three-way meeting to resolve the matter.[10] Sara Mayfield, who grew up with Zelda in Alabama, believed that Zelda "was looking for some momentary diversion rather than for a passionate attachment." She interviewed Jozan almost fifty years later and reported that Jozan believed "Zelda was merely flirting with him to make Scott jealous."[11] Biographer Sally Cline describes Scott making light of the incident in July, something he surely could not have done had he believed that Zelda was rejecting him for Jozan.[12] It has been reported that Fitzgerald awakened the Murphys one night that summer to seek their help after Zelda took too many sleeping pills, which would seem to indicate that Zelda took the matter very seriously indeed, although whether the sleeping-pill incident occurred remains uncertain.[13]

In late October, Fitzgerald sent *The Great Gatsby* to Scribners; shortly afterward, the Fitzgeralds moved to Rome, hoping again to find a less expensive setting. They resided at the Hôtel des Princes, but things did not go well. Fitzgerald drank heavily and was involved in an altercation with the police, later incorporating the beating he received into his novel *Tender Is the Night*. In a letter to his agent, Harold Ober, in January 1925, Fitzgerald vehemently stated his hatred for the country and its inhabitants.[14] His attitude toward his surroundings surely was not helped by Zelda's undergoing an operation in December to enable her to become pregnant and subsequently developing an infection that caused abdominal pain for months.

Fitzgerald remained involved with his novel during the stay in Rome, revising in response to suggestions from Max Perkins and debating which title to choose (among those under consideration: "Trimalchio," "Trimalchio in West Egg," "Gold-Hatted Gatsby," "Among Ash Heaps and Millionaires," and "The High-Bouncing Lover," in addition to "The Great Gatsby"). Up until about a month before publication, Fitzgerald was still vacillating about the title, suggesting either "Gold-Hatted Gatsby" or "Trimalchio," the latter name borrowed from the giver of lavish dinners in *The Satyricon* by the first-century Roman satirist Petronius. Perkins stayed with "The Great Gatsby," explaining that it was too late for such a significant change.[15]

With Zelda still sick and the winter in Rome unpleasantly damp, the Fitzgeralds moved yet again in February after Scott had returned the corrected proofs for the novel, this time choosing the Hotel Tiberio on the island of Capri. There Fitzgerald started writing one of his most acclaimed short stories, "The Rich Boy," and Zelda began taking painting lessons.

THE GREAT GATSBY

The Great Gatsby was published on April 10, 1925. It appeared in a first printing of just under 21,000 and sold for $2. The first printing earned its author something in excess of $6,000, but the sales proved disappointing to Fitzgerald. It clearly was not the blockbuster he had hoped it would be.

The reviews, however, with some exceptions, were quite positive. H. L. Mencken, in the *Baltimore Evening Sun,* expressed little regard for the plot but argued that what "gives the story distinction ... is the charm and beauty of the writing." In *The Saturday Review,* William Rose Benét wrote that "The Great Gatsby reveals thoroughly matured craftsmanship. It has structure. It has high occasions of felicitous, almost magic, phrase." Gilbert Seldes referred to *The Great Gatsby* in *The Dial* as "one of the finest of contemporary novels." Thomas Caldecot Chubb in *The Forum* called Fitzgerald's latest book "the most brilliant novel of the younger generation." Conrad Aiken, one of the most astute readers of the novel, expressed appreciation in the *New Criterion* for *The Great Gatsby* as a novel that "by grace of one cardinal virtue, quite escapes the company of most contemporary American fiction—it has excellence of form." Aiken's analysis of the novel continued with a perceptive explication of its tragic dimensions including the slow unfolding of Gatsby's character, which makes the tragedy personally affecting to the reader.[16]

Despite Fitzgerald's misgivings about the final title, it brilliantly and simply states the essence of Gatsby. He is great in the way that tragic heroes from the time of Aristotle have often been defined: someone of gifts and accomplishments beyond the level of most mortals but at the same time possessor of a tragic flaw that leads to a terrible, disastrous mistake. This error precipitates a reversal of fortune often expressed in terms of a fall from greatness. Ultimately, the tragic hero recognizes the reason for this reversal of fortune, but the recognition brings no real relief.[17]

Jay Gatsby, born James Gatz, reveals his story to narrator Nick Carraway, Gatsby's next-door neighbor, in pieces, Fitzgerald cleverly parceling out information to the reader at the same time. Not until the luxurious party to which Nick has been invited does he meet Gatsby face-to-face. Nick finds himself chatting with another man about their war experiences when Nick refers to Gatsby, and Gatsby, to Nick's embarrassment, identifies himself as the host.

This party is the focal point of chapter 3, but the party scene offers much more than an opportunity for readers to revel vicariously in the type of grandiose parties characteristic of upper-class life on Long Island in the 1920s. One of the most illustrative moments of the novel occurs when Nick and Jordan Baker wander into the library of Gatsby's house and discover a drunken "middle-aged man with enormous owl-eyed spectacles" staring at the books:

> "Absolutely real—have pages and everything. I thought they'd be a nice durable cardboard. Matter of fact they're absolutely real...."
>
> "See!" he cried triumphantly. "It's a bona fide piece of printed matter. It fooled me. This fella's a regular Belasco. It's a triumph. What thoroughness! What realism! Knew when to stop too—didn't cut the pages. But what do you want? What do you expect?"[18]

The man with owl-eyed glasses recognizes the theatrical nature of Gatsby's library, a quality that extends to the entire house and to Gatsby's whole life. It is all a dramatic performance, including the party, put on without regard to expense. The Belasco reference is to David Belasco, a highly popular playwright, director, and producer still alive at the time. His approach to drama included detailed stage settings, integration of music into the production, and subtle use of lighting effects, all character-istics of the party as Fitzgerald describes it. The fact that the pages were not slit for reading enhances Gatsby's stature for the owl-eyed observer who sees better than anyone else at the time just what Gatsby is: someone who is producing a play. As a producer, there is no need to prepare the books for reading; certainly Gatsby himself is too much a man of action to spend time reading much beyond the newspapers that he had been following for years "'just on the chance of catching a glimpse of Daisy's name.'"[19]

As Nick and the reader will learn, Gatsby has acquired his wealth and taken this grand house across the water from Tom and Daisy Buchanan's home as part of his effort to win back the woman he had loved years before, a woman who also is Nick's "second cousin once removed."[20] Gatsby's great production is thus designed for an audience of one, Daisy. The parties exist only for her, given with the hope that some evening Daisy will wander into one of them.

Gatsby as a type of Belasco, though, does not merely wait passively, hoping. He selects his actors, gives them their script, and directs them toward performances that will contribute toward the final effect, tragic though that effect will turn out to be. So at the same party later in the evening, Gatsby, fulfilling his directorial role, summons Jordan. What Gatsby and Jordan discuss is not revealed to the reader and to Nick until the following chapter when Nick goes into New York City with Gatsby, encounters Meyer Wolfshiem, and meets Jordan. It is then that Nick learns from Jordan of Gatsby's past relationship with Daisy—of how Gatsby was forced to leave her behind when he went to war, and of his delayed return from overseas, with Daisy in the meantime having married Tom Buchanan.

What Jordan shares with Nick, though, is not just information. She also has a request from Gatsby: "'He wants to know—' continued Jordan '—if you'll invite Daisy to your house some afternoon and then let him come over.'"[21] Nick complies, which sets in motion the subsequent events: Gatsby and Daisy's reunion in chapter 5, the cessation of parties (the reason for them now ended), the climactic confrontation between Gatsby and Tom in chapter 7, the death of Tom's mistress by a car Daisy is driving (with Gatsby willingly taking the blame), and Gatsby's murder.

As with classical tragedy, the fall from greatness is not death itself, but a fall that precedes death, that ultimately exists irrespective of whether death follows it. For Gatsby, the fall occurs in chapter 7 in a hotel suite in New York. Like two prizefighters trading punches, Gatsby and Tom exchange verbal assaults, the prize Daisy. For a time, Gatsby seems to be winning; he asserts that Daisy loves him, that she has never loved Tom—and finally, Daisy acknowledges also her love for Gatsby. Yet Gatsby is not satisfied. Daisy must state that she never loved Tom, a statement tantamount to affirming that she has been living a lie. It is all too much for her: "'Oh, you want too much!' she cried to Gatsby. 'I love you now—isn't that enough? I can't help what's past.' She began to sob helplessly. 'I did love him once—but I loved you too.'" The small adverb "too" shocks Gatsby: "'You loved me *too?*' he repeated."[22]

Then the pendulum shifts. Tom goes on the offensive, Gatsby finds himself defending himself, and the battle is lost. It is lost because Gatsby cannot compromise and accept Daisy's current love for him. He must have his entire dream, and that dream is rooted in the conviction that one can repeat the past, wiping out the intervening years, and returning the world to a happier time. Nick, far more rooted in realism, more capable of compromise, has earlier tried to convince Gatsby of the nature of things, that one cannot repeat the past:

> "Can't repeat the past?" he cried incredulously. "Why of course you can!"
>
> He looked around him wildly, as if the past were lurking here in the shadow of his house, just out of reach of his hand.
>
> "I'm going to fix everything just the way it was before," he said, nodding determinedly. "She'll see."[23]

Herein lies the tragic error, but it is Fitzgerald's genius, as with the Greek tragedian Sophocles, to make his hero's source of heroism and source of failure identical.[24] What has sustained Gatsby throughout the years, giving him the strength and determination to attain all that he has accomplished, is the unshakable, uncompromising commitment to his dream: to recapture Daisy, to return to life as it was when the young soldier first met and loved her in Louisville, and then to continue from there. Had Gatsby been able to compromise, he surely long before would have yielded to the realism of a Nick Carraway, realized that one cannot repeat the past, and sought a new life without Daisy. Thus, it is his unyielding devotion to what Nick calls Gatsby's "incorruptible dream"[25] that has carried him to the threshold of victory, but it also pushes him too far, into demanding that Daisy acknowledge that her life with Tom had no meaning, in essence had never existed. He gives everything to that incorruptible dream, and it is the dream that brings him close while also making him ultimately fail.

In terms of his dream, Gatsby is dead when he leaves the hotel. The ultimate murder of Gatsby is a kind of narrative mercy killing on Fitzgerald's part. It is inconceivable that Gatsby could lose Daisy, which is to say, his dream, and continue. "What a grotesque thing a rose is," Nick imagines Gatsby thinking as he lies on his pneumatic mattress floating idly in his pool, waiting for a telephone call from Daisy that will never come, waiting for the "ashen figure gliding toward him" that will end his suffering.[26] If recognition of his failure, possibly even of his dream's inevitable failure, ever occurred for Gatsby, it likely did so then.

Still, there is always something grand in greatness, even tragic greatness, as Nick recognizes when he offers his judgment on Gatsby. The last time that Nick sees Gatsby alive is the morning following the death of Myrtle. Unable to sleep, Nick rises early and walks over to Gatsby's house. They talk for several hours until finally Nick must leave to catch a train into the city. Nick shakes hands with Gatsby and starts to leave, but then pauses and calls back to him: "'They're a rotten crowd,' I shouted, across the lawn. 'You're worth the whole damn bunch put together.'" Nick assures the reader, "It was the only compliment I ever gave him, because I disapproved of him from beginning to end."[27]

Despite Gatsby's illegal background, Nick chooses him over the Buchanans, Jordan Baker, and the crowd that floated about Gatsby. The key to Nick's choice of Gatsby lies in Nick's identification with Gatsby's capacity for dreaming and his faithfulness to that dream. It is in that all-encompassing commitment of self to his dream that Nick recognizes Gatsby's greatness and his superiority to himself. Earlier in the book, after discussing the possibility of repeating the past, Nick recalls something elusive that he had once heard but which he cannot recall.[28]

What Nick cannot quite remember is equally lost to readers, but it is surely something he is reminded of by Gatsby's affirmation of his ability to pursue and capture his dream. Perhaps it is a dream Nick once had, but being a man of much more common sense and practicality than Gatsby, he left behind in the world of illusion. Not for Nick to devote his life to pursing "the green light, the orgastic future that year by year recedes before us."[29] But if Nick will not sacrifice his life on the altar of impossible dreams, he senses the majesty and grandeur of such a sacrifice.

F. Scott Fitzgerald's special genius in this novel, beyond the extraordinary descriptions, compelling accounts of social struggles, and almost perfectly timed narrative pacing, is this realization of the attraction, and ultimately destructive nature, of heroism. "Show me a hero," Fitzgerald once wrote, "and I will write you a tragedy."[30]

In his own life, Fitzgerald exhibited much that was tragic. Whether he also was heroic remains for later consideration.

NOTES

1. Matthew J. Bruccoli, *Some Sort of Epic Grandeur: The Life of F. Scott Fitzgerald*, 2nd rev. ed. (Columbia: University of South Carolina Press, 2002), 179.

2. For further information on Fitzgerald's use of Edward Fuller, see "The Fuller-McGee Case" by Henry Dan Piper and related documents in *Fitzgerald's The Great Gatsby*, ed. Henry Dan Piper (New York: Scribners, 1970), 171–84.

3. F. Scott Fitzgerald, *The Great Gatsby*, preface and notes by Matthew J. Bruccoli (New York: Collier Books, 1992), 78.

4. David Pietrusza, *Rothstein: The Life, Times, and Murder of the Criminal Genius who Fixed the 1919 World Series* (New York: Carroll & Graf, 2003), 148.

5. The photo with note is reproduced in *Some Sort of Epic Grandeur*, 180.

6. Ibid., 528.

7. *The Short Stories of F. Scott Fitzgerald,* ed. Matthew J. Bruccoli (1989; New York: Scribners, 1995), 252; *The Great Gatsby,* 162.

8. *The Short Stories of F. Scott Fitzgerald,* 271.

9. *The Notebooks of F. Scott Fitzgerald,* ed. Matthew J. Bruccoli (New York: Harcourt Brace Jovanovich, 1980), entry 839.

10. Nancy Milford, *Zelda: A Biography* (New York: Harper & Row, 1970), 110–12.

11. Sara Mayfield, *Exiles from Paradise: Zelda and Scott Fitzgerald* (New York: Delacorte, 1971), 95–98.

12. Sally Cline, *Zelda Fitzgerald: Her Voice in Paradise* (New York: Arcade Publishing, 2002), 150.

13. See, for example, Cline, *Zelda Fitzgerald,* 153–54.

14. *F. Scott Fitzgerald: A Life in Letters,* ed. Matthew J. Bruccoli (1994; New York: Simon and Schuster, 1995), 94.

15. For a discussion of the choice of title and various substantive revisions to the novel, see *Some Sort of Epic Grandeur,* 206–16.

16. For these and many other comments about *The Great Gatsby,* including some minority, negative opinions, see the set of reviews in *F. Scott Fitzgerald in His Own Time: A Miscellany,* ed. Matthew J. Bruccoli and Jackson R. Bryer (New York: Popular Library, 1971), 345–65.

17. Among the multitude of books on Greek tragedy, two that remain especially useful are H. D. F. Kitto's *Greek Tragedy: A Literary Study,* 3rd ed. (1939; London: Methuen, 1970) and *The Cambridge Companion to Greek Tragedy,* ed. P. E. Easterling (New York: Cambridge University Press, 1997).

18. *The Great Gatsby,* 49–50.

19. Ibid., 84.

20. Ibid., 10.

21. Ibid., 83.

22. Ibid., 140.

23. Ibid., 116–17.

24. For important studies of Sophocles's tragedies, see C. M. Bowra's *Sophoclean Tragedy* (Oxford: Clarendon Press, 1967) and Gordon MacDonald Kirkwood's *A Study of Sophoclean Drama* (1958; Ithaca, NY: Cornell University Press, 1994).

25. *The Great Gatsby,* 162.

26. Ibid., 169.

27. Ibid., 162.

28. Ibid., 118.

29. Ibid., 189.

30. *The Notebooks of F. Scott Fitzgerald,* entry 316.

F. Scott Fitzgerald is shown here at age three with his father, Edward Fitzgerald. *Credit: Photofest.*

Fitzgerald's sister, Annabel, appears with their parents, Edward and Mollie, in this photo. *Credit: Photofest.*

Fitzgerald in 1911. At 15 he was enrolled as a student in the Newman School. *Credit: Photofest.*

Fitzgerald appears at the bottom left, weating his beanie as part of freshman initiation at Princeton. *Credit: Photofest.*

This is a publicity photograph show-ing Fitzgerald, a Princeton junior, dressed as a chorus girl to advertise the Triangle Club's *The Evil Eye*. Fitzgerald wrote the lyrics for the show, but academic difficulties made him ineligible to participate in its winter tour. *Credit: Photofest*.

The author and his young wife, both styl-ishly attired, were at the peak of their social success in the early 1920s. *Credit: Photofest*.

This photo of Fitzgerald was taken
at the time of *The Great Gatsby*
when his literary reputation was high
and his future seemingly unlimited.
Credit: Photofest.

Fitzgerald in the mid-1930s—his
"crack-up" years. *Credit: Photofest.*

Chapter 6

BUILDING TOWARD THE CRASH: THE END OF THE 1920S AND ZELDA'S FIRST BREAKDOWN (1925–1930)

The second half of the 1920s drew F. Scott and Zelda Fitzgerald toward a breakdown that paralleled, although in different terms, the financial collapse of 1929 that ushered in the Great Depression. For the Fitzgeralds, money would be a factor in their downward spiral but not the primary cause of their troubles. Instead, alcoholism, mental illness, Scott's inability to write consistently, and marital strife would draw the once glittering embodiments of the Roaring Twenties into their own personal collapse.

Indications of the couple's difficulties were present throughout these years; in fact, as has been pointed out earlier, warning signs had been present from the beginning of their relationship. *The Great Gatsby* serves as a demarcation point between the period when Fitzgerald, despite his difficulties, especially with drink and money, was an extremely productive writer, and the second half of the decade when his problems finally interfered significantly with his writing career. During the first half of the 1920s, Fitzgerald published three novels that brought him international acclaim; more than forty short stories, some of which remain American classics; a play that, although entertaining, failed to achieve the level of success of his fiction; and a variety of articles and book reviews. It would be almost a decade after *Gatsby*, though, before Fitzgerald would publish a fourth novel, and he would not live to complete his fifth.

FITZGERALD AND HEMINGWAY

With the Fitzgeralds in Paris during the spring of 1925, Scott had the opportunity to meet the younger writer, Ernest Hemingway, whose early career he had been enthusiastically following. The meeting inaugurated one of the most famous literary friendships in American history, although the relationship would become too complex and ambivalent to sustain an easy label of friendship; nor would it ultimately prove beneficial to Fitzgerald.

Much of what is known about the early meetings between the two writers comes from Hemingway's book of Paris memoirs, A *Moveable Feast*, begun in 1957 but not published until 1964, three years after Hemingway's death. There are several problems with accepting Hemingway's account of events, including the delay of some thirty years during which his recollection of those events may have faltered. In addition, Hemingway, always deeply concerned with his own image, seems to have presented events from a perspective that helped convey a personally flattering view of himself. Readers should seriously consider the suggestion that Hemingway offers in the preface, that the book may be read as fiction, although the reality is that the book also contains much that is historically correct.[1]

One does not get far into Hemingway's description of the first meeting between the writers, one world famous, the other aspiring to fame, in the Dingo Bar on the rue Delambre in Montparnasse before encountering a factual error. Fitzgerald's supposed companion, a former Princeton baseball player named Dunc Chaplin, almost surely was not in Paris at the time.[2] The error is a small matter, but it should put the reader on alert. Hemingway's physical description of Fitzgerald is composed with careful attention to effect, demonstrating condescension combined with fondness.

Throughout the memoir, Hemingway adopts the tone of a kindly parent trying his best to take care of a talented but immature child whose problems are partly caused by himself, partly by a jealous wife. In the Dingo Bar account, Fitzgerald is presented as possessing "a face between handsome and pretty," with "a delicate long-lipped Irish mouth that, on a girl, would have been the mouth of a beauty ... and a handsome, almost beautiful, unmarked nose." A "pretty face" further subverts the description.[3] None of this is positive from Hemingway's point of view: the pretty face, the feminine mouth, the nose unmarked by such Hemingway manly pastimes as boxing. And the conclusion of the paragraph, in which Hemingway notes that Fitzgerald's mouth worried him then, and even more so after getting to know him, exhibits Hemingway's ability to merge humor and criticism, both at Fitzgerald's expense.

The account further finds fault with Fitzgerald for his inappropriately personal questions, especially a query as to whether Hemingway had slept with his wife before marriage, a question that implies Fitzgerald's

supposed concerns about his own sexual adequacy described later in
A Moveable Feast. Fitzgerald also comes off badly for his inability to hold
his drink. As the evening progressed, Fitzgerald's face came to resemble,
in Hemingway's words, "a death mask," and he needed help getting into
a taxi for his ride home.[4]

Not long after the initial meeting, Hemingway accompanied Fitzgerald
to Lyon to retrieve the Fitzgeralds' Renault, which had been left to
have the top removed. Hemingway was enthusiastic about going with
Fitzgerald, but as he describes it the return trip turned difficult when
rain forced them to stop at a hotel. Scott supposedly became convinced
that he had a temperature, and Hemingway, in his account, turns the
incident into a comic farce. Playing the father role, Hemingway reassures
Fitzgerald that he is fine but later sends a waiter out for a thermometer
to reassure Fitzgerald. When the waiter returns with a large bath thermometer, Fitzgerald eyes it suspiciously, wondering where to place it.
Hemingway, thinking quickly, tells him under the arm and then promptly
takes Fitzgerald's temperature, announcing the registered temperature as
normal. To prove the matter, he takes his own temperature and shows
Fitzgerald the same reading, not letting on that the thermometer is
broken and cannot read anything other than what it currently shows.[5]

Within a day or two of the Lyon trip, Fitzgerald took Hemingway a
copy of *The Great Gatsby.* Hemingway recalls in *A Moveable Feast* liking
the novel a great deal, but even his praise is tinctured with condescension.
After removing the dust jacket, which Hemingway considered garish and
in bad taste, he read the book. Hemingway records that after finishing the
novel he resolved to overlook Fitzgerald's behavior and be a true friend
to him because, having written such a good book, he undoubtedly could
write an even finer one. As Hemingway points out, that conclusion was
before he met Zelda and therefore "did not know the terrible odds that
were against him."[6]

The relationship between Hemingway and Zelda immediately turned
hostile, Hemingway blaming Zelda for trying to keep Scott from writing
because of her jealousy at his success, and Zelda viewing Hemingway
as a fake. Each questioned the other's sexual orientation, Hemingway
accusing Zelda of deliberating flirting with women to make Scott jealous,
and Zelda labeling Hemingway a fraud, a "professional he man, a pansy
with hair on his chest."[7] Zelda's animosity toward Hemingway became so
strong that in 1929 she charged her husband with having a homosexual
relationship with him.[8] The accusation, thoroughly false, probably grew
out of her increasing mental instability as much as her extreme dislike
for Hemingway. If Hemingway's assertion that he discerned madness in

Zelda as early as 1925 is to believed, he was certainly prescient regarding her mental health.[9]

Zelda's accusations toward her husband included the charge that his penis was too small to give her sexual pleasure, a particularly devastating attack that Hemingway records in A Moveable Feast in the section entitled "A Matter of Measurements." The incident apparently occurred in 1929. While finishing lunch with Hemingway at Michaud's restaurant, Fitzgerald shared with Hemingway his wife's accusation that his failure "was a matter of measurements." He added that the charge bothered him a great deal and that he needed to know if her observation were accurate. Again Hemingway reduces the traumatic to the level of farce, inviting Fitzgerald into the restroom for a quick physical examination, pronouncing Fitzgerald "perfectly fine," and then suggesting a trip to the Louvre to compare himself with its male statues.[10]

During the summer of 1925, Fitzgerald wrote one of his finest short stories, "The Rich Boy," about the wealthy Anson Hunter and the superiority that Hunter felt toward others. The story appeared in two parts in the January and February 1926 issues of Red Book. Fitzgerald continued to revise the story for inclusion in his third collection of short stories, All the Sad Young Men, which was published in February 1926 and included such additional Fitzgerald masterpieces as "Winter Dreams" and "Absolution." Otherwise, he accomplished little during the year, doing some planning but apparently no actual writing on a fourth novel.[11]

The Fitzgeralds spent part of the summer of 1925 on the Riviera at Cap d'Antibes enjoying their friendship with Gerald and Sara Murphy. Any difficulties between the Fitzgeralds seemed not to affect their daughter. Although Scottie regularly was under the supervision of nannies, both parents lavished considerable affection on her. Fitzgerald tried to be strict but could seldom bring himself to administer any punishment, much preferring to play games with her. Zelda drew upon her considerable artistic talents to make paper dolls and playhouses for her daughter. Scottie later remembered being especially happy during the years she spent in France with her parents, an exception being the catechism classes that her father required her to attend on Sundays.[12]

Fitzgerald at the time was continuing to recruit Hemingway, who was completing his first novel, The Sun Also Rises, for Scribners, an association that Hemingway also coveted. However, Hemingway's three-book contract with Boni & Liveright, agreed to prior to the publication of In Our Time in 1925, guaranteed Boni & Liveright the opportunity to publish Hemingway's next book. There was an out, though, for the author. If the publisher declined the next offering, the contract was rendered void.

After finishing the first draft of *The Sun Also Rises*, Hemingway set it aside to work on another book, one that he would call *The Torrents of Spring*. According to Hemingway biographer Michael Reynolds, the new book had two objectives: to induce a rejection from Boni & Liveright and establish the author's fictional independence from novelist Sherwood Anderson, who had encouraged and assisted the younger author in a variety of ways over the previous few years. Also a Chicago-area author, Anderson was widely viewed as something of a mentor to Hemingway.[13]

The Torrents of Spring, which Hemingway dashed off in ten days, placed Boni & Liveright in an untenable position because it parodied Anderson, perhaps the publisher's most prestigious author. The alternatives were either to insult and perhaps lose its widely popular star or risk losing a promising but not yet established new writer. The publisher chose the latter, Horace Liveright rejecting the manuscript in a lengthy, carefully modulated letter that placed much of the blame for the rejection on a reading public that lacked the capacity to appreciate a cerebral satire.[14] The decision freed Hemingway to follow Fitzgerald's urging, which by that time had been matched by welcoming overtures from Scribners editor Max Perkins.

If Fitzgerald was pleased by Hemingway's opportunity to join him at Scribners, he could not have been entirely happy with his friend writing him into *The Torrents of Spring*. In an "Author's Note to Reader," Hemingway writes that Fitzgerald arrived one afternoon and "suddenly sat down in the fireplace and would not (or was it could not, reader?) get up and let the fire burn something else so as to keep the room warm."[15] The reference to Fitzgerald's indulgence in alcohol, however, apparently did not draw an overt reaction from Fitzgerald.

Perkins accepted both of Hemingway's books in February 1926 without having seen *The Sun Also Rises*, which was not mailed to Scribners until late April. Fitzgerald read a copy in June and responded with a lengthy detailed critique suggesting a number of changes. Hemingway followed much of his advice, most notably cutting lengthy background material from the beginning of the novel.[16] Hemingway later claimed in *A Moveable Feast* that he had not shown Fitzgerald the novel until after the revised and shortened version had been delivered to Scribners. In the same passage, he flatly stated that he did not want any help from Fitzgerald while he was rewriting the novel.[17] These statements demonstrate Hemingway's unwillingness, or inability, to acknowledge help and his penchant for rewriting the past to declare his own self-sufficiency.

HOLLYWOOD AND LOIS MORAN

Scott and Zelda returned to the United States in December 1926, spending Christmas with Zelda's family in Montgomery and visiting Scott's parents, who had moved to Washington, D.C. Their search for a place to live was put on hold when Fitzgerald received a job offer from United Artists to write a comedy that would star Constance Talmadge. Scott and Zelda left Scottie with his parents during their approximately two months in Hollywood at the beginning of 1927. His writing efforts proved unsuccessful, as the script, entitled "Lipstick," was rejected. Fitzgerald never found writing for the movies a congenial role, as he considered it artistically a lesser form of writing than his novels and something to do primarily for the money. Nor did he thrive within the group-concept approach to writing that working for the films entailed.

The time in Hollywood put new strains on their marriage, as Zelda became jealous of Scott's interest in a young actress named Lois Moran who had achieved stardom with her performance in *Stella Dallas* in 1925. Although there was no physical relationship between Fitzgerald and the actress, they were attracted to each other. Fitzgerald even underwent a screen test with the idea of making a film with her. Zelda's jealousy took concrete form when she burned some of her clothes in a bathtub and, on the train back East, threw out of a window the expensive wristwatch that Scott had given her in 1920.

Despite his Hollywood failure, Fitzgerald gained two important characters for later fiction. Lois became the model for the young actress, Rosemary Hoyt, a major character in Fitzgerald's next novel, *Tender Is the Night*. Also during his stay in California, Fitzgerald met the youthful directing genius, Irving Thalberg, head of production at Metro-Goldwyn-Mayer. Thalberg would serve as the model for Monroe Stahr in *The Last Tycoon* (now often referred to as *The Love of the Last Tycoon: A Western*), the unfinished novel Fitzgerald was working on when he died.[18]

ELLERSLIE AND ZELDA'S BALLET

The Fitzgeralds, with the help of Scott's former Princeton roommate, John Biggs, Jr., found a home to rent in March 1927 that appealed to them at Edgemoor in the Wilmington, Delaware, area. Called "Ellerslie," the large, imposing two-story house was fronted by four heavy columns facing a long drive and was surrounded by lawns that reached down to the Delaware River. Much larger than necessary for a family of three, it nonetheless came relatively cheaply at $150 per month and provided convenient access to New York City by way of a two-hour train trip. Fitzgerald hoped that the location would provide him with a good writing environment.

Zelda, during the two years spent at Ellerslie, threw herself into creative activity on a number of fronts, including finding appropriate furniture for their new home. Throughout their married life together, the Fitzgeralds had always rented, usually in apartments or houses already furnished, consequently accumulating little in the way of furniture. Furnishing their new home thus proved a challenge, one that Zelda partly met by purchasing oversized furniture. Visitors may have felt like children once they dropped into the huge couches and chairs, but the stratagem helped to fill up the mansion's many large rooms.

Zelda also resumed ballet dancing in the summer of 1927, an activity she had enjoyed growing up in Montgomery. Unfortunately, she approached ballet with the unrealistic goal of becoming a top ballerina, a virtual impossibility for anyone resurrecting the dance at twenty-seven after years away from it. Zelda went into Philadelphia three times weekly to take lessons from Catherine Littlefield, who directed the Philadelphia Opera Ballet Corps and had herself taken lessons from the acclaimed Madame Lubov Egorova of the Diaghilev Ballet Russe. The latter would soon come to figure prominently in Zelda's life.

Zelda also returned to writing, selling three articles during 1927 ("The Changing Beauty of Park Avenue" to *Harper's Bazaar*, "Looking Back Eight Years" to *College Humor*, and "Editorial on Youth" to *Photoplay*). In writing, though, she inevitably took second place to her husband, so much so that even most of her own published efforts appeared with a dual byline to enhance sales.

Zelda was widely talented, her skills including painting, writing, dance, and crafts (including the creations she fashioned for Scottie). However, in no one area had she come close to achieving the level of success enjoyed by Scott in writing. Her desire to mark out her own area of excellence, perhaps fueled by jealousy of Lois Moran, who visited Ellerslie soon after the Fitzgeralds moved in, contributed to her resumption of ballet lessons and the ardor with which she threw herself into the activity.

Success was seriously occupying Zelda's thoughts at the time, witnessed by her reflections in the essay "Looking Back Eight Years." A retrospective evaluation of the Jazz Age generation, the piece asks what that generation has accomplished now that its members have entered their thirties. "Success was the goal for this generation," Zelda writes, adding that to a great extent they have reached the goal. Yet even that success has proved unsatisfying, the essay notes, for "what they really wanted is something deeper and richer than that."[19] By many standards, Zelda had enjoyed success: marriage to a famous author, motherhood, fame and fortune (albeit fortune that dissipated as quickly as it came), even some publishing credits of her own. But Zelda had not won that "something deeper and richer," her own personal identity established through her own individual proof of excellence. Ballet offered that opportunity, or so she thought.

As Zelda turned increasingly to ballet, Scott resumed writing short stories, producing five pieces for the *Saturday Evening Post*. Lois Moran supplied inspiration for "Jacob's Ladder" as a youthful department store clerk turned into a movie star with the help of a man in his thirties, who then chooses fame on the screen over the man's love. The other *Post* stories were "The Love Boat," "A Short Trip Home," "The Bowl," and "Magnetism." Unfortunately, Fitzgerald made little headway on his novel.

RETURN TO PARIS

The Fitzgeralds returned to Paris in April 1928. Zelda, who had increased her practicing to several hours daily, looked forward to beginning lessons with Lubov Egorova. Her commitment to ballet increasingly made her unavailable for the partying that both had enjoyed throughout their marriage, causing Fitzgerald to go out by himself. His resentment added fuel to the alcoholic fire, and his behavior while drinking led to two jailings during the summer.

With progress on the novel still slow and needing money for the Paris trip, Fitzgerald once again turned to short stories, producing the remarkable set of stories about the Fitzgerald-like character Basil Duke Lee for *The Saturday Evening*. The stories are highly effective, but Fitzgerald feared that his reputation as a serious novelist would suffer if he published a collection of stories about children and therefore long resisted reissuing the Basil stories, and the five later Josephine Perry stories, in book form. Recognizing that both his reading audience and the critics were awaiting his next novel, Fitzgerald wanted a serious, adult masterpiece to follow *The Great Gatsby* and hoped that the book on which he had been working for several years would fulfill their, and his, expectations.

"The Freshest Boy" and the other Basil stories were not written as chapters but nonetheless offer considerable coherence in character development. Fitzgerald carefully worked out Basil's growth from the age of eleven in "That Kind of Party" to college at Yale in "Basil and Cleopatra." Other characters also reappear, such as Lewis Crum in "The Freshest Boy" and "He Thinks He's Wonderful," Brick Wales in "The Freshest Boy" and "Basil and Cleopatra," Hubert Blair in "The Scandal Detectives" and "A Night at the Fair," and Minnie Bibble in "He Thinks He's Wonderful" and "Forging Ahead." The reappearances highlight Basil's character traits and reflect significant changes he has undergone over the years.[20]

The Fitzgeralds returned to the United States in October 1928, Fitzgerald bringing along a Paris taxi driver, Philippe, to serve not only as his chauffeur and general servant but also as his all too often drinking partner. He found it as easy to be arrested for disorderly conduct with Philippe as without him and would call on his lawyer friend John Biggs to get them released.

Fitzgerald also resumed his association with Hemingway. On November 19, Scott and Zelda attended a Princeton-Yale football game with Hemingway and Pauline Pfeiffer, whom Hemingway had married the previous year after his divorce from his first wife, Hadley. Also in the party was Henry Strater, a painter and former Princeton friend of Fitzgerald's. The game went well, Princeton winning 12–2, but the excursion was not without incident. The five took a train from Princeton to Philadelphia, where Philippe met them. The Buick kept overheating on the drive to Ellerslie, but Scott and Zelda would not let Philippe stop to check the water or oil. Fitzgerald became drunk that evening, and the following morning he caused Hemingway much worry about missing his train to Chicago by insisting that everyone play croquet.

Just a few weeks later, on December 6, Hemingway was en route by train from New York to Key West, Florida, when he received a telegram informing him that his father had died. Not expecting to need much money until he reached his destination, Hemingway found himself in need of cash in order to change his plans and go immediately to Chicago. Always generous, Fitzgerald responded to an urgent telephone call from Hemingway and wired $100 to the North Philadelphia station.[21]

At about the same time as these encounters with Hemingway, Fitzgerald was writing one of his most famous short stories, "The Last of the Belles." The story is set in Tarleton, Georgia, also the setting for the earlier "The Ice Palace," which depicts the first of Fitzgerald's Southern belles, Sally Carrol Happer. As with "The Ice Palace," "The Last of the Belles" chronicles the relationship between a beautiful Southerner and a Northern suitor, even reintroducing Sally Carrol Happer in a supporting role. The suitor, like the young Fitzgerald when he met Zelda, is a Yankee soldier stationed in the South during World War I. Andy meets and is captivated by Ailie Calhoun, but after the war he moves on to Harvard Law School and a career seemingly having little to do with the law—building commercial airplanes. He returns after six years, hoping, like Gatsby, to repeat the past and reclaim his youth; however, unlike Gatsby, he both discovers and is willing to admit that the past is over with.

"The Last of the Belles" would be the final time that Fitzgerald returned in his fiction to Southern women within a thematic context of love, glamour, and youthful dreams, a fictional decision reflective of the increasing evaporation of romance and grandeur from his relationship with Zelda. That the earlier heroine reappears marks both stories clearly as bookends for a fictional shelf consigned to the author's past.

If Fitzgerald had needed confirmation that his relationship with Zelda had badly deteriorated, he needed to look no farther than his own home to observe his wife obsessively practicing her ballet techniques before a large gilt mirror to the endless repetitions of "The March of the Toy Soldiers." So committed was she to her practicing that she would dance even through meals while Scott and their guests dined. Zelda also returned to painting, mingling one obsession with another as she repeatedly labored hour after hour at the canvas depicting ballet scenes.[22]

A BOXING MATCH

The Fitzgeralds returned again to Europe in the spring of 1929, a stay that would do nothing to halt their decline. Not long after arriving in Nice, Fitzgerald was arrested for disorderly conduct. Zelda's unrelenting determination to succeed in ballet, meanwhile, was becoming increasingly expensive, leading her to plan a series of stories to pay Lubov Egorova's fees, which had reached $300 per month. *College Humor* published five stories starting in July and running through January 1931 but insisted on listing the usual joint byline for most of them. One of the stories, "The Southern Girl," borrows from Fitzgerald's "The Last of the Belles" as well as "The Ice Palace," featuring a relationship between a Southern belle and a Northern soldier and having the young woman discover, during a visit to the young man's midwestern home, that the relationship will not work.

Fitzgerald was continuing to struggle with his novel, dropping the matricide theme that had served as an important element in the story (involving a young American who murders his mother) and establishing the role of Rosemary Hoyt based on Lois Moran. If the novel progressed slowly, Fitzgerald still had the ability to write short stories rapidly, producing seven during 1929 for *The Saturday Evening Post*. His stories increasingly drew upon troubling aspects of his marriage, including a wife in "Two Wrongs" who turns to ballet as her husband's health declines through alcoholism and tuberculosis. The stories brought a raise in compensation to $4,000 per story, the highest dollar figure Fitzgerald's short stories would earn.

An incident during the summer of 1929 shook the Fitzgerald-Hemingway friendship with lasting consequences. Hemingway was in Paris completing his novel A *Farewell to Arms* and deliberately avoiding Fitzgerald because he wanted to work without dealing with Fitzgerald's drunken behavior, inevitable disruptions in Hemingway's working habits, and suggestions for improving Hemingway's newest novel. Fitzgerald, understandably, was hurt by his friend's aloofness and clearly recognized the reversal in reputation that the two authors had undergone since the mid-1920s: Hemingway climbing the ladder of success to the point where he was probably the most widely acclaimed American author, Fitzgerald stumbling down the same ladder.

The incident involved a boxing match. Hemingway and a Canadian writer named Morley Callaghan, one of many authors Fitzgerald had recommended to Scribners, enjoyed boxing against each other in Paris, and Fitzgerald wanted to be part of the action. Finally, he was invited to attend a match as timekeeper. As the action heated up in the second round, Fitzgerald became so engrossed that he lost track of the time. When Callaghan knocked Hemingway down, Fitzgerald was so shocked at seeing Hemingway fall that he blurted out that he had let the round go too long. Hemingway, perhaps embarrassed to have an observer see him get knocked down, responded with a vicious verbal assault on Fitzgerald, accusing him of deliberately letting the round go long because he wanted to see Hemingway beaten. Fitzgerald was taken aback by the accusation, but things soon settled down, leaving only Fitzgerald still shaken by the event.

The incident likely would have ended there were it not for a newspaper article in the *New York Herald Tribune* in November falsely stating that Callaghan had knocked Hemingway out. Callaghan immediately sent the paper a correction. However, Fitzgerald, concerned about what Hemingway would think of the exaggeration in the *Tribune*, rather than waiting for Callaghan to act contacted him with an urgent directive to correct the story. Callaghan was upset that Fitzgerald would assume he would not correct the story on his own, while Hemingway suspected that Callaghan might have been behind rumors that Hemingway was a homosexual and planted the story to further harm his reputation. As a result, despite Max Perkins's attempt to reconcile his three authors, the friendship with Callaghan was over and the relationship between Fitzgerald and Hemingway, although still intact, was frayed.

ZELDA'S FIRST BREAKDOWN

As the world hurtled toward the financial collapse of October 29, 1929 (forever after known as "Black Tuesday"), and onset of the Great

Depression, Zelda's behavior continued to deteriorate. In October, Zelda grabbed the steering wheel while Scott was driving and tried to send the car over a cliff. On another occasion, she claimed that flowers at a market were communicating with her. As 1929 yielded to the new decade, Zelda developed bronchitis, but despite a high fever insisted on continuing her ballet lessons with Egorova because she felt safe only while dancing. Meanwhile, she had started painting flowers, but far from conventionally beautiful, they stretched across the canvas in contorted shapes.

With guests over for lunch one day in March 1930, Zelda became terrified that she would miss her lesson and dashed from the table. One of the guests, Oscar Kalman, drove her in a taxi while Zelda changed clothes in the back seat. When Oscar found himself in a traffic jam, Zelda leapt from the taxi and raced on foot to the studio. The proverbial "straw" occurred the following month when Zelda returned to their apartment in such a disturbed state that a guest, the playwright Michael Arlen, urged visiting a clinic. At that point, there seemed no alternative to seeking professional help. Zelda's first breakdown had been coming for a long time; on April 23, 1930, about three weeks after the Fitzgeralds' tenth wedding anniversary, Zelda entered the Malmaison Clinic near Paris.[23]

Fitzgerald noted in his *Ledger* summary for the year September 1929–September 1930 his own personal relationship to what his country was experiencing financially: "The Crash! Zelda and America."[24] The world ultimately would recover from the Great Depression, but a total recovery for the Fitzgeralds from their own private crash would be beyond their reach.

NOTES

1. Ernest Hemingway, *A Moveable Feast* (1964; New York: Macmillan, 1987).

2. Matthew J. Bruccoli, *Some Sort of Epic Grandeur: The Life of F. Scott Fitzgerald*, 2nd rev. ed. (Columbia: University of South Carolina Press, 2002), 225.

3. Hemingway, *A Moveable Feast*, 149.

4. Ibid., 151–52.

5. Ibid., 154–75.

6. Ibid., 176.

7. Ibid., 181; Sara Mayfield, *Exiles from Paradise: Zelda and Scott Fitzgerald* (New York: Delacorte, 1971), 141.

8. Nancy Milford, *Zelda: A Biography* (New York: Harper and Row, 1970), 153.

9. Hemingway, *A Moveable Feast*, 186.

10. Ibid., 189–90.

11. For a detailed examination of the twelve drafts that *Tender Is the Night* went through, see Matthew J. Bruccoli, *The Composition of* Tender Is the Night: *A Study of the Manuscripts* (Pittsburgh: University of Pittsburgh Press, 1963).

12. Eleanor Lanahan, *Scottie The Daughter of . . .: The Life of Frances Scott Fitzgerald Lanahan Smith* (New York: HarperCollins, 1995), 38–40.

13. Michael Reynolds, *Hemingway: The Paris Years* (1989; New York: Norton, 1999), 334.

14. Walker Gilmer, *Horace Liveright: Publisher of the Twenties* (New York: David Lewis, 1970), 123–25.

15. Ernest Hemingway, *The Torrents of Spring* (1926; New York: Scribners, 1972), 76.

16. Bruccoli, *Some Sort of Epic Grandeur*, 146–50; Michael Reynolds, *Hemingway: The American Homecoming* (Cambridge, MA: Blackwell, 1992), 40–42.

17. Hemingway, *A Moveable Feast*, 184–85.

18. Bruccoli discusses the alternate titles for Fitzgerald's final novel in *Some Sort of Epic Grandeur*, 463–64.

19. Zelda Fitzgerald, *The Collected Writings*, ed. Matthew J. Bruccoli (1991; New York: Macmillan, 1992), 408.

20. A helpful discussion of the Basil and Josephine sequences by Jackson R. Bryer and John Kuehl occurs in the introduction to *The Basil and Josephine Stories*, ed. Bryer and Kuehl (New York: Scribners, 1973), vii–xxvi.

21. Scott Donaldson, *Hemingway vs. Fitzgerald: The Rise and Fall of a Literary Friendship* (Woodstock, NY: Overlook, 1999), 120–22.

22. Sally Cline, *Zelda Fitzgerald: Her Voice in Paradise* (New York: Arcade Publishing, 2002), 213–28.

23. Cline, *Zelda Fitzgerald*, 256–59.

24. *F. Scott Fitzgerald's Ledger: A Facsimile*, edited by Matthew J. Bruccoli (Washington, DC: NCR/Microcard Editions, 1972).

Chapter 7

STRUGGLING TO ENDURE: *TENDER IS THE NIGHT* AND THE DISINTEGRATION OF A MARRIAGE (1930–1934)

Paris in springtime is usually as romantic a setting as one can find, but it was far from that for F. Scott and Zelda Fitzgerald in 1930. Zelda entered Malmaison Clinic in great distress, lamenting her absence from her ballet practice and calling frantically for her teacher, Madame Egorova. The early evaluation of Zelda noted her identity problems, especially fear that she might be a homosexual, a concern seemingly based on her passionate feelings toward Egorova. In retrospect, Zelda's passion appears to have been more an obsessive desire to please her instructor by becoming an accomplished ballerina than sexual. Her veneration for Egorova was also tied up with her own feeling that only ballet gave her life meaning.[1]

ZELDA AT PRANGINS

Zelda left Malmaison on May 11, but her health was no better. Her efforts to resume ballet led to hallucinations in which she saw horrific phantoms; she also attempted suicide. Eleven days after her departure from Malmaison, Zelda entered Val-Mont Clinic at Gilon, Switzerland. The Val-Mont physician, Dr. H. A. Trutmann, noted her fear that both she and her husband might be homosexual as well as her obsession with returning to her ballet lessons. Because the clinic was not a psychiatric institution, Dr. Oscar Forel, who operated a psychiatric clinic, Les Rives de Prangins, at Nyon on Lake Geneva, was brought in to consult on Zelda's condition. On June 4, she left Val-Mont, agreeing to enter Dr. Forel's clinic.

When Zelda changed her mind about continuing treatment, Scott called on her brother-in-law, Newman Smith, who with Zelda's sister Rosalind was living in Brussels, Belgium. Smith helped persuade Zelda to accept treatment at Prangins. Asking for Smith's help was not easy for Fitzgerald, as Rosalind and the rest of the Sayre family blamed his drinking for causing Zelda's emotional problems. Fitzgerald represented Rosalind's attitude and his own guilt and worries about his daughter in "Babylon Revisited," which he wrote in December 1930. In the story, Charles Wales's sister-in-law, Marion Peters, blames her sister Helen's death on Wales and short-circuits his attempt to reclaim custody of his daughter, Honoria.

The loss of a daughter is entirely fictional, as Fitzgerald remained in charge of Scottie and emotionally close to her through all of the family's difficulties. During Zelda's stay at Prangins, he commuted between Paris and Switzerland in order to be near Zelda while also maintaining a careful watch on Scottie. A governess helped considerably, especially during his absences.

Fitzgerald was a prolific letter writer during this period, regularly exchanging letters with Zelda and writing to Dr. Forel with suggestions for treatment. Scott and Zelda found it easier to express fondness for each other in letters than in person because face-to-face meetings often produced unpleasant scenes. For example, Fitzgerald brought Scottie to Prangins for Christmas, but the visit did not go well. Zelda became upset and broke the Christmas tree ornaments. Fitzgerald tried to salvage the holiday season for Scottie by taking her skiing at Gstaad. As she did to her husband, Zelda wrote loving letters to Scottie, repeatedly expressing her desire to be with her.

Dr. Forel believed that Zelda's recovery required her abandoning ballet, a position with which Fitzgerald concurred. Consequently, Fitzgerald wrote to Egorova in June 1930 asking for an assessment of Zelda's dancing ability. Both men expected Egorova to cooperate with a negative evaluation that would convince Zelda to abandon her efforts to become a professional dancer.

Instead they received a balanced judgment that was more positive than they wanted but still served to discourage Zelda. According to Egorova, Zelda had the potential to dance professionally but had started her training too late to become a star. While praising Zelda, she ranked a number of her other students as superior. Zelda took the report hard and abandoned her dream of dancing professionally but continued dancing for her own pleasure once released from Prangins.[2]

ALCOHOLISM

Dr. Forel tolerated Fitzgerald's suggestions for treating Zelda but believed it would not be possible to effect a cure for Zelda without also treating

Fitzgerald. Forel believed that Fitzgerald also needed to abandon a habitual practice, his drinking. As an alcoholic, Fitzgerald may have been unable to stop drinking without help anyway, but he did not try. Instead, he argued that his drinking had not caused Zelda's problems and that to quit would be to forego a normal source of pleasure while accepting blame for what had not been his responsibility. To what extent this rationale was an alcoholic's justification for continuing to drink is hard to say. Fitzgerald at least convinced himself that he had a right, even a duty, to continue drinking.

Over the next few years, though, Fitzgerald did attempt to control his drinking. He was hospitalized for alcoholism and other health problems at Johns Hopkins Hospital nine times between 1932 and 1937. After Fitzgerald's first hospitalization, Dr. Benjamin Baker established a routine intended to make him at least stop and think before drinking. Whenever Fitzgerald wanted a drink, he was to telephone Baker, an ultimately unsuccessful regimen that testifies to Dr. Baker's idealism and capacity for self-punishment. Other strategies that Fitzgerald devised included reserving certain times of the day for sobriety (and writing his novel) and rationing his drinking to one ounce of gin per hour (a method that failed when he started borrowing against future hours).

In a letter to Max Perkins after the 1934 publication of *Tender Is the Night*, Fitzgerald acknowledged that drinking had delayed finishing the novel. A short story can be written while drinking, he explained, but "for a novel you need the mental speed that enables you to keep the whole pattern in your head and ruthlessly sacrifice the sideshows.... If a mind is slowed up ever so little it lives in the individual part of a book rather than in a book as a whole; memory is dulled."[3]

Despite Fitzgerald's refusal to attempt a complete stop to his drinking, he put great time and energy into attempting to assist with Zelda's recovery. In addition to his visits and letters, he worked hard to pay for Zelda's treatment, including the fees for Dr. Paul Eugen Bleuler, who had named schizophrenia and was the leading authority on the illness. Bleuler consulted with Dr. Forel and confirmed a diagnosis of schizophrenia. Bleuler offered hope of recovery and reassured Fitzgerald that he had not caused Zelda's illness.

Fitzgerald, as was his practice when needing quick money, put aside his novel in favor of short stories. His writings during 1930–31 included the five-story sequence about Josephine Perry based on his first love, Ginevra King. The stories take the Chicago debutante emotionally downward until, in the final story, "Emotional Bankruptcy," she has reached the state noted in the title, with no emotion left for the man she desires. Although intellectually she understands and assures Edward Dicer that he is everything she has ever wanted, she admits that she cannot feel anything. Throughout the story, financial terms convey Josephine's psychological state: seeing invitations, for example, as "overdue bills," realizing that "one cannot both spend and have," and recognizing the emotional emptiness that resulted from spending her emotional capital too early and too quickly.[4]

The metaphors reflect Fitzgerald's own self-reflections as well as his worries about paying for Zelda's treatment. In "Babylon Revisited," Charles Wales also expresses his losses (his dead wife, separation from his daughter, health problems, and temporary confinement in a sanitarium), which he associates with his reckless living prior to the stock-market collapse of 1929, in financial terms. The barman at the Ritz Hotel comments about Wales's financial loss during the crash. Wales acknowledges the loss but adds that he lost everything that he valued during the boom. "Selling short," the barman wonders. "Something like that," Wales answers.[5]

In Paris during June 1930, Fitzgerald met a new Scribners author, Thomas Wolfe, who had recently published *Look Homeward, Angel,* and whose later novels would include *You Can't Go Home Again.* Fitzgerald was impressed with Wolfe's ability and praised him to their joint editor, Max Perkins. Wolfe, though, was unimpressed, viewing Fitzgerald as a perpetual college boy who had never completely grown up.[6] Wolfe later changed his opinion after reading *Tender Is the Night,* which he considered Fitzgerald's best work.[7]

Fitzgerald's father, Edward, died of a heart attack on January 26, 1931, forcing Fitzgerald to leave Zelda and return alone to the United States for the funeral at St. Mary's Church in Rockville, Maryland. Fitzgerald took the death hard. In an unfinished essay entitled "The Death of My Father," he expressed his love for his father and acknowledged his indebtedness to him for all he had learned about life prior to meeting Monsignor Fay. The reminiscence includes a touching account of Fitzgerald running away on the Fourth of July when he was seven and receiving a spanking when he returned. Then his father brought him outside and they watched the fireworks together. After the fireworks, Scott asked his father to tell a story, and he complied with one about his favorite subject, the old South.[8]

While in the United States, Fitzgerald visited the Sayres in Montgomery to report on Zelda. The trip was difficult, as the family continued to blame him for Zelda's illness, even accusing Fitzgerald of institutionalizing Zelda to get rid of her.

Zelda made good progress during Fitzgerald's absence, improving to the point where she was able to go skiing at St. Cergues. Trips with Fitzgerald to Geneva and Montreaux in Switzerland followed, and Zelda expressed high spirits both in person and in letters to Scott and Scottie. The three of them went to the Lake Annecy region in southern France for two weeks in July, enjoying tennis, fishing, dancing, and eating in the cafés.

In May 1931, Fitzgerald's mother, Mollie, came to Paris for a visit, and in August the Fitzgeralds visited Gerald and Sara Murphy in the Austrian Tyrol. Patrick, one of the Murphy children, was suffering from tuberculosis, and Fitzgerald became angry when he thought that Scottie had bathed in water he had used. That turned out not to be true, and Fitzgerald used the scene in *Tender Is the Night*. Patrick, the youngest of the three Murphy children, died in January 1937, almost two years after the older son, Baoth, had caught measles at a boarding school and died suddenly when a mastoid infection developed requiring surgery, which led to bacteria in the spinal fluid and spinal meningitis.[9] Only the Murphy daughter, Honoria, survived into adulthood.

RETURN TO AMERICA AND HOLLYWOOD

Zelda was discharged from Prangins on September 15, 1931. Shortly afterward, the Fitzgeralds returned to the United States, sailing on the *Aquitania*, the ship on which the newly married couple had first traveled to Europe a decade before with the whole world seemingly at their feet.

Despite the Sayres' hostility toward Fitzgerald, he and Zelda decided to live in Montgomery, where Zelda might feel more at ease. They rented a house, and Fitzgerald returned to his novel. Zelda also was busy writing that fall, both before and after leaving Prangins. She produced several stories, including "A Couple of Nuts." The story, published in *Scribner's Magazine* in 1932, is about a young American couple, Larry and Lola, who reflect Zelda's sense of deterioration in her marital relationship. High-spirited singers and musicians, they perform successfully in France during the 1920s but become corrupted by the wealthy with whom they associate, until "where there had been something pleasant and clean and crisp as an autumn morning now there was nothing."[10] Larry ends up drowning when a yacht goes down in a storm, with only Lola surviving. Destitute but hopeful that she may get a job in a new musical show, she writes to the story's narrator asking for money.

Fitzgerald planned to work hard on his novel and stay close to Zelda while she continued to recuperate, but an offer from Hollywood proved too financially enticing to turn down. Metro-Goldwyn-Mayer (MGM) invited Fitzgerald to rewrite a screenplay based on Katherine Brush's novel *Red-Headed Woman*. The film was to star the original "Blonde Bombshell," Jean Harlow. Irving Thalberg, the "boy wonder" head of production at MGM, wanted Fitzgerald, whom he had met during Fitzgerald's previous trip to Hollywood in 1927, and offered $1,200 per week for six weeks. Fitzgerald reluctantly accepted, going out to California in November.

As with his earlier screenwriting effort, this one also proved unsuccessful. He made $6,000, and although the film was made, Fitzgerald's screenplay was not used. The low point of his stay, at least in his own mind, was a Sunday party at the home of Thalberg and his wife, actress Norma Shearer. Feeling out of place and drinking too much, Fitzgerald tried to prove he belonged by performing his "Dog" song with actor Ramon Navarro accompanying him on the piano. The performance was not well received, some guests even booing him. Fitzgerald's embarrassment was at least partly assuaged by Norma Shearer's telegram the next day saying how much she enjoyed his presence. Fitzgerald wrote the incident into the short story "Crazy Sunday."

While Fitzgerald was in Hollywood, Zelda's father, who had never recovered from influenza he contracted the previous spring, died. Although Zelda initially appeared to hold up well, Judge Sayre's death removed a rock of stability from Zelda's life. Growing up, she had rebelled against his authority, but then and later she had always felt able to count on his permanence. An attack of asthma signaled the return of Zelda's emotional problems. Fitzgerald returned to Alabama for Christmas and took Zelda to Florida in January, hoping that the climate change might ease her asthma. She developed eczema on her neck, another sign of her emotional distress, and on the train back to Montgomery drank a great deal and woke Scott up early in the morning complaining of frightening things being done to her.

ZELDA'S SECOND BREAKDOWN AND *SAVE ME THE WALTZ*

When the return to Montgomery did not help, Zelda was admitted to the Henry Phipps Psychiatric Clinic of the Johns Hopkins University Hospital in Baltimore on February 12. Dr. Adolf Meyer, director of the clinic and an authority on schizophrenia, and Dr. Mildred Squires allowed Zelda to paint and work on a novel, believing both activities to be therapeutic.

Zelda completed the novel, *Save Me the Waltz*, by March. Unfortunately, it precipitated a great deal of discord between her and Scott. Assuming her husband's disapproval because of the novel's heavy autobiographical content, Zelda sent the manuscript to Max Perkins at Scribners before giving Fitzgerald a copy. Fitzgerald reacted angrily, accusing Zelda of stealing material that he considered his, and doing so while he had delayed his novel in order to raise money for her medical treatment. Among his complaints were Zelda's appropriation of crucial episodes from his work-in-progress and her use of the name "Amory Blaine," the name of the main character in Fitzgerald's first novel, *This Side of Paradise*. Fitzgerald raised these concerns in a letter to Dr. Squires, to whom Zelda dedicated the novel; he also wired Max Perkins, urging him not to act on the novel until he received a revision.

Zelda responded to Fitzgerald with protestations of love and unwillingness to do anything that would offend him. While she tried to smooth over the dispute and mollify Fitzgerald for not having shown him the novel before submitting it to Perkins, she still claimed equal right to their joint experiences even as she agreed to make the revisions her husband demanded. By March 25, Fitzgerald was telling Perkins to move ahead with publishing the novel subject to impending revisions. Fitzgerald was sufficiently satisfied with Zelda's changes by May 14 that he praised the novel highly to Perkins. In the same letter, he acknowledged the "subtle struggle" between Zelda and Hemingway (certainly an understatement) and urged Perkins not to discuss the novel with Hemingway for fear he might resent any of Perkins's attention being directed toward Zelda's book.[11]

Save Me the Waltz was published in October 1932. It neither sold well nor received a favorable critical reception, as Zelda's heavily descriptive and ornamental style makes the book a cumbersome read. Nonetheless, it is of interest because, despite the revisions, it remains consistently autobiographical. The novel features Alabama Beggs, daughter of a judge, who falls in love with and marries a Northern painter named David Knight. Knight's quick success, the couple's notoriety in New York, a daughter named Bonnie, trips to the Riviera and Paris, Alabama's infatuation with a French pilot, the husband's affair with an actress, Alabama's attempt to forge a ballet career, an illness (blood poisoning rather than mental illness) that ends Alabama's dancing career, and a host of other details draw on actual people and events in Scott and Zelda's life together.

LA PAIX

To be closer to Zelda, Fitzgerald rented a fifteen-room Victorian home named La Paix at Towson near Baltimore in May 1932. Edgar Allan Poe, a cousin of the famous writer, was the lawyer who helped Fitzgerald find La Paix and also handled his legal matters. Poe was an 1891 Princeton graduate and, as a star quarterback for the Princeton eleven, an All-American in 1889.

La Paix was owned by Bayard Turnbull, an architect, and his wife, Margaret. Fitzgerald grew close to Margaret, discussing books with her and sharing his concerns about rearing Scottie properly. Fitzgerald spent a great deal of time at La Paix with Scottie and the Turnbull children (Eleanor, Francis, and Andrew), teaching them to dive, shoot a .22 rifle, and play a variety of historical games with Greek and Roman soldiers he had bought for Scottie in France. He also participated in card tricks and plays with the children and talked football with young Andrew Turnbull. Andrew remembered those years fondly and almost thirty years later wrote a biography of Fitzgerald.[12]

Zelda was gradually able to increase the amount of time she spent away from Phipps at La Paix with Fitzgerald and Scottie. On June 26, she was discharged from Phipps, but unlike her discharge from Prangins, leaving the institution brought with it no confidence of a cure. Fitzgerald realized that she probably would never be completely healthy. In fact, for the rest of her life, Zelda was never far from hospitalization and was periodically in need of medical attention.

Hoping to avoid renewed conflicts about literary ownership of their marriage, Fitzgerald encouraged Zelda to return to painting. She complied, creating paintings of ballet dancers with enlarged feet and legs, symbolic of her anguish over losing her ballet dream, although she continued dancing privately at La Paix. Zelda developed considerable skill as a painter and had an exhibition of some of her paintings and drawings in New York from March 29 to April 30, 1934, at a gallery owned by Cary Ross, whom the Fitzgeralds had meant in Paris. Among the paintings was a portrait of Fitzgerald, *The Cornet Player*, which the writer Dorothy Parker bought. At the same time, the Hotel Algonquin featured a smaller exhibit.

While the Fitzgeralds were trying to resume family life at La Paix, Fitzgerald faced new financial challenges. He wrote several stories for *The Saturday Evening Post* in 1932, but the price for his stories dropped steadily from $4,000 to $2,500, their 1925 level. Depression-era economics were a factor, but so was the magazine's growing dissatisfaction with the quality of Fitzgerald's stories. In August of that year, Fitzgerald made his first visit to Johns Hopkins Hospital for treatment of his medical problems, including alcoholism.

Amid the challenges Fitzgerald faced regarding Zelda's health and their financial state, he made a final push to complete the novel that had inched ahead haltingly over the better part of a decade. Fitzgerald hired a full-time secretary, Isabel Owens, to help with the typing. He wrote longhand in pencil and she typed sections of the novel as he completed them. Owens typed the manuscript triple-spaced to give Fitzgerald more room to make revisions and produced, in addition to the ribbon copy, two carbon copies. Fitzgerald then revised multiple copies and had Owens retype the best version. As he worked on the novel, he also went through various titles: *The Drunkard's Holiday, Doctor Diver's Holiday: A Romance*, and finally *Tender Is the Night: A Romance*.

Despite his determination to finish the novel, Fitzgerald spent considerable time with Scottie and Zelda. They played chess, tennis, croquet, and word games, and Fitzgerald introduced Scottie to his own favorite childhood books. His mother occasionally visited from Washington, where she and her husband had moved several years before Edward's death.

In addition, Zelda continued writing. She abandoned another novel when Fitzgerald again complained about her using his material. Instead she focused on a play, completing *Scandalabra* in October 1932. The play employs reverse psychology, as a wealthy man wills his money to a nephew on condition that the nephew live a scandalous and irresponsible life. The nephew and his wife attempt to comply but grow tired of their lifestyle and decide to live in a moderate, responsible manner, which was the uncle's objective from the beginning. After substantial shortening and rewriting by Fitzgerald, the play, produced by a group called the Junior Vagabonds, ran for six nights in Baltimore during the summer of 1933.

Also during this time, Fitzgerald organized his *Notebooks* into twenty-three sections that included ideas and passages for future writing. In March 1933, the *Post* published his essay "One Hundred False Starts" about the difficulties of the writer's life, the "feeling of utter helplessness" that sometimes overtakes him, and his desire "to get in a good race or two when the crowd is in the stand."[13]

May 1933 brought Fitzgerald one of the low points in his marriage to Zelda. A three-way discussion at La Paix among Fitzgerald, Zelda, and Dr. Thomas Rennie, a psychiatrist from Phipps, covered so much ground that the stenographer required 114 pages to type the dialogue. Subjects included Fitzgerald's drinking, his claim to own his and Zelda's shared experiences, and his insistence on controlling what Zelda wrote. Fitzgerald was so angry about the exchange that he discussed with Poe the possibility of divorcing Zelda.

Fitzgerald did not pursue a divorce, but in September he lost someone else close to him—Ring Lardner, who died of a heart attack on September 25 at the age of forty-eight, an end hastened by alcoholism. Fitzgerald had once told Max Perkins that he was Hemingway's alcoholic as Lardner was his, a statement that inadequately conveyed the real fondness Fitzgerald felt for Lardner.[14] In October, Fitzgerald wrote a moving tribute for his old friend from his Great Neck days for the *New Republic*. In the account, he laments Lardner's failure to realize his potential, partly because of his preoccupation with "a few dozen illiterates playing a boy's game" (referring to Lardner's baseball writings) but concludes his judgement of Lardner by noting simply that "a great and good American is dead."[15]

TENDER IS THE NIGHT

Finally, *Tender Is the Night* was completed. Fitzgerald delivered the manuscript to Scribners in late October 1933. After a vacation with Zelda in Bermuda in November, during which he became ill with pleurisy, Fitzgerald, Zelda, and Scottie moved in December from La Paix to a townhouse on Park Avenue in Baltimore.

The novel was serialized in *Scribners Magazine* in four installments from January to April 1934. Fitzgerald continued revising the novel during its magazine appearance. On April 12, 1934, Scribners published the novel in book form. It sold reasonably well, quickly running through a first printing of 7,600 copies, with two more printings following during the spring. Nonetheless, the book did not achieve the financial blockbuster status that its author wanted and needed. During the years he had been working on the novel, Fitzgerald borrowed heavily from Scribners against the book's sales and from his agent, Harold Ober, against the anticipated income from its magazine appearance. Fitzgerald also had borrowed from his mother, and the income from *Tender Is the Night* proved insufficient for Fitzgerald to get out from under all of his debts.

Fitzgerald had moved away from the matricide theme in the novel to focus on an American psychiatrist, Dick Diver, whose marriage to one of his patients, Nicole Warren, precipitates a personal and professional decline in Diver. The relationship borrows heavily from Fitzgerald's own life with Zelda and his concerns about his professional career. Diver also is partly based on Gerald Murphy, especially early in the novel, although the parallel is primarily confined to issues of social grace and behavior.

Other characters also are drawn from people Fitzgerald knew, but the finished products usually are composites. Rosemary Hoyt is a young actress with parallels to Lois Moran, but the relationship between her and Diver is more sexual and complex than that between Fitzgerald and Moran. Elements of Edouard Jozan and Ring Lardner are incorporated into Tommy Barban and Abe North, respectively, but most of what the characters do is fictional.

Tender Is the Night was generally well received, but not without qualification. The long wait for the successor to *The Great Gatsby* had created high expectations, while Fitzgerald's long struggle to complete the novel had hindered his ability to keep the whole story in focus. There were some complaints that Dick Diver's character was inconsistent and the reasons for his decline insufficiently clear. Fitzgerald himself grew to regret the structure of the novel with its long flashback to Diver's meeting with Nicole, then a patient at a Swiss clinic, believing that the novel might have fared better with readers and critics if he had followed a strict chronological approach throughout. There also is a shift in point of view. Book 1 is told largely from Rosemary Hoyt's perspective. The novel then focuses on Dick Diver in books 2 and 3.[16]

Malcolm Cowley's review in the *New Republic* introduced a perspective on Fitzgerald that has retained considerable importance: his ability simultaneously to be within and without, both actively participating in an event and able to store up details of the event for future writing as if he were an observer—both, in Cowley's words, "a guest at the ball" and "a little boy peeping in through the window." For Cowley, though, this dual focus is a "divided personality" that had come to be an impediment to a clear perspective on his subject. Other readers are likely to see this dual status as an extraordinary talent that permitted both emotional immediacy and descriptions characterized by perceptive observations and rich details.[17]

Despite its imperfections, *Tender Is the Night* added considerably to Fitzgerald's enduring status as one of America's greatest writers. As Hemingway grew to appreciate the novel more with time, so subsequent history has generally treated the novel well as an intellectually and aesthetically mature work of art. If not the equal of *The Great Gatsby*, it remains Fitzgerald's second greatest novel, with only the unfinished promise of *The Love of the Last Tycoon* competing for that honor.

Publication of *Tender Is the Night* was not the only conclusion in 1934 to a long process of struggle. In February, Zelda suffered her third breakdown. Probably contributing to her relapse was the suicide of her brother, Anthony Sayre, Jr., in August 1933.[18] Suffering badly from depression, he leaped out of a hospital window to his death. Zelda's third breakdown clearly ended any remaining residue of hope for anything approaching a full recovery. On February 12, she returned to the Phipps Clinic, from where she was transferred in March to Craig House at Beacon, New York. It was during Zelda's stay at Craig House that the New York exhibitions of her art occurred. As her condition worsened, she was moved to the Sheppard and Enoch Pratt Hospital near Baltimore on May 19, although the major reason for the move was financial. The Pratt Hospital cost less than Craig House, and the Fitzgeralds were in trouble financially. Zelda worried about how much her illness was costing and tried to help by writing two short essays, "Show Mr. and Mrs. F. to Number—" and "Auction—Model 1934," for *Esquire*. Both appeared during the summer.

Zelda readily accepted moving to the less expensive hospital but was frightened of its barred windows and locked doors and offended by her initial treatment, which included a body search, confiscation of her clothes, and a bath with a disinfectant solution. She suffered badly from guilt, feeling that she had ruined her husband's life, and endured hallucinations during which she thought that she heard Fitzgerald's voice. Zelda pleaded in letters for his love and even attempted to strangle herself.[19]

Both Scott and Zelda often found themselves in despair. In her essay "Auction—Model 1934," Zelda writes of an imaginary auction, but as she unpacks the crates of their possessions accumulated over the years she finds that most objects are too broken or battered for sale, fit only to be consigned to the attic. Concerning that period of time, Fitzgerald wrote, "I left my capacity for hoping on the little roads that led to Zelda's sanitarium.[20]

NOTES

1. See chapter 16 of Sally Cline's *Zelda Fitzgerald: Her Voice in Paradise* (New York: Arcade Publishing, 2002), 247–65, for a discussion of Zelda's sexuality.

2. Egorova's evaluation is available in Matthew J. Bruccoli, *Some Sort of Epic Grandeur: The Life of F. Scott Fitzgerald*, 2nd rev. ed. (Columbia: University of South Carolina Press, 2002), 302.

3. *The Letters of F. Scott Fitzgerald*, ed. Andrew Turnbull (1963; New York: Dell, 1965), 259–60.

4. *The Short Stories of F. Scott Fitzgerald*, ed. Matthew J. Bruccoli (1989; New York: Simon and Schuster, 1995), 556, 560.

5. *The Short Stories of F. Scott Fitzgerald*, 633.

6. Bruccoli, *Some Sort of Epic Grandeur*, 306–07.

7. *Correspondence of F. Scott Fitzgerald*, ed. Matthew J. Bruccoli and Margaret M. Duggan, with Susan Walker (New York: Random House, 1980), 332.

8. "The Death of My Father" is reprinted in *The Apprentice Fiction of F. Scott Fitzgerald: 1909–1917*, ed. John Kuehl (New Brunswick, NJ: Rutgers University Press, 1965), 177–82.

9. Honoria Murphy Donnelly, with Richard N. Billings, *Sara and Gerald: Villa America and After* (1983; New York: Holt, Rinehart and Winston, 1984), 88–91.

10. *Zelda Fitzgerald: The Collected Writings*, ed. Matthew J. Bruccoli (1991; New York: Macmillan, 1992), 362.

11. For these communications, see *Correspondence of F. Scott Fitzgerald*, 288–94, and *F. Scott Fitzgerald: A Life in Letters*, ed. Matthew J. Bruccoli (1994; New York: Simon and Schuster, 1995), 209–19.

12. Andrew Turnbull, *Scott Fitzgerald* (New York: Scribners, 1962).

13. *Afternoon of an Author: A Selection of Uncollected Stories and Essays*, ed. Arthur Mizener (1957; New York: Scribners, 1958), 127–36.

14. *F. Scott Fitzgerald: A Life in Letters*, 226.

15. *The Crack-Up,* ed. Edmund Wilson (1945; New York: New Directions, 1956), 34–40.

16. See Bruccoli, *Some Sort of Epic Grandeur,* 363–70, for an overview of critical reactions to *Tender Is the Night* and *F. Scott Fitzgerald in His Own Time: A Miscellany,* ed. Matthew J. Bruccoli and Jackson R. Bryer (New York: Popular Library, 1971), 370–92, for a selection of reviews.

17. *F. Scott Fitzgerald: In His Own Time,* 387–90.

18. For a discussion of Anthony's death and its effect on Zelda, see Kendall Taylor, *Sometimes Madness Is Wisdom: Zelda and Scott Fitzgerald: A Marriage* (New York: Ballantine Books, 2001), 278–80.

19. See Cline, *Zelda Fitzgerald,* 349–52, for Zelda's first days at Sheppard-Pratt.

20. *The Notebooks of F. Scott Fitzgerald,* ed. Matthew J. Bruccoli (New York: Harcourt Brace Jovanovich, 1980), entry 1362.

Chapter 8

THE CRACK-UP PERIOD: FITZGERALD HITS BOTTOM (1934–1937)

Fitzgerald began a series of stories in April 1934 about a ninth-century French aristocrat named Philippe, the Count of Villefranche. Desperately needing money, he hoped to profit twice from his work by writing the series as stories that he could sell separately to magazines but also use as sections of a historical novel. Fitzgerald envisioned Philippe as a medieval version of Hemingway, although parallels are hard to identify.[1]

FITZGERALD'S CREATIVE DETERIORATION

Redbook Magazine bought the first four Philippe stories, publishing three ("In the Darkest Hour," "The Count of Darkness," and "The Kingdom in the Dark") between October 1934 and August 1935. The magazine's declining interest in the series and the stories' disappointing quality brought Fitzgerald's plan for a novel about the character to a halt. *Redbook* held the fourth story, "The Gods of Darkness," until November 1941, apparently publishing it then to capitalize on whatever interest the author's recent death might have sparked in his writings.

As Fitzgerald's alcoholism continued to take its toll, his ability to fashion short stories declined, leading to a gradual shift from *The Saturday Evening Post* to *Esquire* as his primary magazine market. As the *Post* editors complained about the quality of his stories, Fitzgerald established a strong relationship with *Esquire*'s editor, Arnold Gingrich. Gingrich admired Fitzgerald's work, but the magazine paid only a fraction of what the *Post* had been offering, a maximum of $250 per piece. The first Fitzgerald publications in *Esquire* were Zelda's essays "Show Mr. and Mrs. F. to Number—" and

"Auction—Model 1934," which Scott polished, and which appeared under a dual byline during the spring and summer of 1934.

Fitzgerald's initial *Esquire* publication, "Sleeping and Waking," appeared in the December issue, the first in a series of autobiographical essays that ran in the magazine through August 1936. The modest remuneration from these essays required Fitzgerald to search out other avenues for making money. He approached his former Princeton professor Christian Gauss, then Dean of the College, about presenting a series of lectures on writing fiction. Gauss, perhaps concerned about Fitzgerald's drinking and uncertain of his reliability, declined university sponsorship, suggesting instead that he speak to a club, an alternative that Fitzgerald declined.

Fitzgerald's income for 1934 was slightly over $20,000, but just $58.35 came from his book royalties although his books were still in print and would remain so until his death.[2] With his short stories failing to produce the steady income they had generated in the past, he relied ever more heavily on borrowing, yet even that proved less reliable. Scribners declined additional advances against books that the publisher clearly could not count on. Fitzgerald continued borrowing from his editor, Max Perkins, as well as from his agent, Harold Ober, his Princeton roommate, John Biggs, Jr., and his own mother.

Scribners maintained its practice of following Fitzgerald's novels with a collection of short stories, publishing *Taps at Reveille* in March 1935. The volume included five Basil Duke Lee stories, three stories featuring Josephine Perry, and such soon-to-be classics as "Crazy Sunday," "The Last of the Belles," and "Babylon Revisited." Despite the overall quality of the collection, it received only one printing and did little to remedy its author's financial plight.

The years 1935 and 1936 were extremely difficult for both Scott and Zelda. Zelda remained suicidal throughout 1935, once running from her husband directly toward nearby railroad tracks. Fitzgerald caught up with her before she could throw herself under an oncoming train.[3]

Fitzgerald felt his own health deteriorating and moved to Tryon, North Carolina, to seek treatment for his tuberculosis. He stayed at the Oak Hall Hotel, depositing Scottie with friends Nora and Maurice "Lefty" Flynn, who lived in the area. Nora was a sister to Lady Astor, who in 1919 became the first woman to serve in the British House of Commons, and Lefty was a former actor with, like Fitzgerald, a serious alcohol problem. Fitzgerald based one of his last well-paying short stories, "The Intimate Strangers," which he sold to *McCall's* for $3,000 in 1935, on the Flynns.

Fitzgerald and Scottie returned to Baltimore after about two weeks, but Fitzgerald returned in May to North Carolina, residing at the Grove Park

Inn in Asheville. There he developed a close friendship with Laura Guthrie, whom he hired as a typist. He confided in her and they went to movies together, but their relationship remained platonic. It was not so with a wealthy woman from Texas, Beatrice Dance, also residing at the inn, with whom Fitzgerald had a short-lived affair. Fitzgerald broke off the affair in August by means of a long explanatory letter. He enclosed a letter Zelda had sent him, according to biographer Matthew Bruccoli, in June.[4] One of the most widely quoted of the letters from or to Fitzgerald, it is highly nostalgic and self-reproaching. Zelda laments that there was nothing "but an empty shell" to greet him when he visited at Sheppard-Pratt, affirms how good he had been to her, regrets that they had "met in harshness and coldness where there was once so much tenderness and so many dreams," and longs for an idyllic setting with a house surrounded by hollyhocks with Scottie running around happily and Scott "writing books in dozens of volumes."[5]

Fitzgerald's creative efforts were failing with frustrating regularity. He wrote a short radio drama, "Let's Go Out and Play," for the *World Peaceways* program. It aired in October 1935, leading Fitzgerald to plan a thirteen-part radio series about a father and his daughter, but Ober could not sell the project. Another father-daughter plan, a series of stories about a girl named Gwen and her widower father, yielded four stories. The *Post* bought two of them, "Too Cute for Words" and "Inside the House," but rejected two and suggested that Fitzgerald abandon the series. A number of other Fitzgerald stories went unsold during the 1935–37 period, and others were only reluctantly accepted. *Collier's*, for example, finally accepted "Thumbs Up" in 1937 after the story was rejected by thirteen magazines, and only then on condition that it be successfully revised.

Fitzgerald underwent treatment for his tuberculosis from Dr. Paul Ringer in Asheville during the summer of 1935 and was hospitalized because of his drinking. His repeated medical experiences suggested yet another series, this one about a nurse. The *Post* rejected his first effort but took the second story, "Trouble," while making it clear that the magazine did not want any more stories about the character. "Trouble," published in March 1937, was Fitzgerald's final *Post* story, his sixty-fifth in the magazine.

THE CRACK-UP PERIOD

Leaving Scottie with friends, Fitzgerald went to Hendersonville, North Carolina, in November 1935 and rented a room in the Skyland Hotel, settling into possibly the lowest point of his life, often referred to as his "crack-up" period after a series of extremely personal, confessional essays that he wrote for *Esquire*. "The Crack-Up," which gave the series its name, appeared in *Esquire* in February 1936 and was followed over the next two months by "Pasting It Together" and "Handle with Care," and by "Author's House" and "Afternoon of an Author" in July and August.

The Crack-Up essays lament the author's declining ability to write, associating the failure with the concept of emotional bankruptcy. Although novels and short stories were proving difficult for Fitzgerald, the essays are outstanding compositions, exhibiting perceptive self-analysis in brilliant, if often tragic, images. In "Pasting It Together" (the title for this essay and for "Handle with Care" mistakenly switched and applied to the wrong essays in *The Crack-Up* volume),[6] Fitzgerald likens himself to a cracked plate but, arguing that decline is not the same as uselessness, notes that a cracked plate may be retained for use. It will not be brought out when company is being served, nor can it go into the dishpan with other plates or it may be broken completely. However, even a cracked plate "will do to hold crackers late at night or to go into the ice box under left-overs."[7]

"Author's House" is written as an interview with an author (Fitzgerald himself), as the author takes the interviewer through his house from cellar to attic, and up to the cupola, from where they can see a river in the distance and hear the wind blowing. The journey through the house also becomes a metaphoric journey through the author's life. "Afternoon of an Author" is written in the third person as a cross between a short story and an autobiographical essay recounting one day in Fitzgerald's life as he goes out for a walk, hoping "to get something out of it professionally" and realizing he needs "reforestation."[8]

There is both pathos and courage in Fitzgerald's description of himself, but many readers, including magazine editors, saw only the pathetic image of a has-been writer. Both Fitzgerald's agent, Harold Ober, and his Scribners editor, Max Perkins, regretted the essays, feeling that they made the task of getting Fitzgerald's fiction into print more difficult. The *Esquire* pieces, though, led Simon and Schuster to propose a volume of autobiographical writings. Perkins resisted both the intrusion of a rival publisher and Fitzgerald's continuation in the confessional mode, suggesting that Fitzgerald instead write a memoir for Scribners. However, neither project materialized.

The most difficult aspect of the Crack-Up essays for Fitzgerald came in August 1936, when Hemingway published his short story "The Snows of Kilimanjaro" in the same *Esquire* issue that included "Afternoon of an Author." Hemingway strongly disliked Fitzgerald's essays, finding the confessional tone unmanly, like crying in public. Apparently believing that a public jolt might get Fitzgerald to stop what Hemingway considered whining and face up to his problems, Hemingway attacked Fitzgerald publicly in the story.

In "The Snows of Kilimanjaro," the dying Harry recalls "poor Scott Fitzgerald" and his awe of the rich. He recalls, in a reference to "The Rich Boy," how Fitzgerald had once begun a story by noting that the rich are different from other people. Hemingway then recalls someone responding to Fitzgerald that the difference is that the rich have more money, and that his recognition that the rich were not a special race had helped to wreck him. The incident never happened to Fitzgerald, although Hemingway had been involved in a similar dialogue with critic Mary Colum, who made the comment about how the rich are different.[9]

The attack came at a particularly bad time for Fitzgerald. Zelda, suffering from religious obsessions, had been transferred to Highland Hospital in Asheville, North Carolina, in April. Zelda believed that the end of the world was near and that she was receiving direct communications from Christ. Her mania resulted in obsessive praying as well as efforts to distribute written comments about God to her friends.[10] In July, Fitzgerald broke his right shoulder while diving into water on an outing with Zelda. The injury, compounded by a fall in his bathroom, added another impediment to writing, as a cast kept his right arm elevated so that he either had to dictate to a secretary or write on a board suspended above him.

To be publicly humiliated by a man he considered a friend greatly upset Fitzgerald, but he retained his composure in responding to Hemingway. Knowing how easy it was to anger him, Fitzgerald adopted an understated, even bantering tone in his letter. He acknowledges Hemingway's good intentions but asks that he excise the references when reprinting the story. Hemingway's response has not survived, but according to Fitzgerald in a September 19 letter to Perkins, Hemingway wrote a rambling, incoherent, "crazy" letter, but agreed to Fitzgerald's request. Perkins later received a letter in which Hemingway claimed to be trying to help Fitzgerald and relayed that information to Fitzgerald. Fitzgerald's correspondence with Perkins conveys his continuing fondness for Hemingway as well as his realization that Hemingway also was not the writer or person he had been, but "like a punch-drunk pug fighting himself in the movies."[11]

Fitzgerald's difficulties clearly did not include an inability to examine himself and Hemingway with reasonable objectivity and considerable acuity. Several years earlier, when Hemingway already had passed him in literary reputation, Fitzgerald wrote in his *Notebooks*, "I talk with the authority of failure—Ernest with the authority of success." The statement is all the more powerful (and sad) for being a private reflection.[12]

Fitzgerald's mother died in September, leaving him only modest relief from his financial troubles. Her estate was valued at just under $23,000, which Fitzgerald had to split with his sister, Annabel. In addition, $5,000 he had borrowed from his mother was removed from his share. Most of his inheritance went to pay off debts, which were so substantial that he also secured money he owed to Ober and Scribners with his $60,000 life insurance policy.

Then, when life seemed unable to get worse, it got worse. A *New York Post* journalist named Michel Mok visited Fitzgerald at the Grove Park Inn in Asheville, to which Fitzgerald had returned in the summer. The interview was planned to coincide with Fitzgerald's fortieth birthday and to discover whether he was really through as a successful writer. Fitzgerald was ill, drinking heavily, and still suffering from the broken shoulder. Mok ingratiated himself with praise for Fitzgerald's writings and induced the author to open up to him.

The article appeared on September 25 on the front page of the *Post* under the headline "The Other Side of Paradise/Scott Fitzgerald, 40,/Engulfed in Despair/Broken in Health He Spends Birthday Re-/gretting That He Has Lost Faith/in His Star." Mok described Fitzgerald's "jittery jumping off and onto his bed, his restless pacing, his trembling hands, his twitching face with its pitiful expression of a cruelly beaten child.... his frequent trips to a highboy, in a drawer of which lay a bottle."[13]

The published article devastated Fitzgerald, who responded by swallowing morphine. Fortunately, the overdose induced vomiting and Fitzgerald suffered no major physical damage from the drug. His shame and anger, though, were reinforced when the article was reprinted in *Time* magazine. Ironically, Fitzgerald turned for help to Hemingway, who had just humiliated him in *Esquire*. Hemingway responded from Montana with his willingness to assist, but there was little he could have done short of going to New York and punching Mok. Fitzgerald quickly realized he had no recourse but to move on and withdrew his request.

FATHER AND DAUGHTER

The fall of 1936 brought at least some good news. Scottie was admitted to the Ethel Walker School in Simsbury, Connecticut. Surely with embarrassment at his financial plight, Fitzgerald secured a discounted tuition rate. By this time, Fitzgerald was already in the habit of sending Scottie letters that combined deep affection with detailed exhortations regarding how she should behave, what she should read, and the importance of studying hard. Academic achievement held primary position in a number of the letters, but he also encouraged her to write to Zelda. A sprinkling of the salutations demonstrates Fitzgerald's tender love for Scottie: "Dear Pie," "Scottina," "Darlin'," "Dearest Scottina," "Dearest Pie," "Darling Scottina." He generally signed the letters "Daddy." Among many tender moments in the letters is Fitzgerald's opening sentence in a letter he sent from Grove Park Inn in the summer of 1935: "It was fine seeing you, and I liked you a lot (this is aside from loving you which I always do)."[14]

Scottie loved her father and knew he was an important man. However, she cared no more for constant instruction than any other teenager would. In addition, she had to endure the added difficulties of her mother's hospitalizations and her father's serious drinking problem. The latter surfaced very publicly on December 22, 1936, at a dance he organized for Scottie at the Belvedere Hotel in Baltimore. He had written to Scottie on December 12 assuring her that the dance would not be extravagant—an orchestra with a hurdy-gurdy (the musician playing it to be accompanied by a dancing monkey) and waltz dancing for Scottie and her friends. He also planned to have a swing orchestra in the next room for the adults.

Unfortunately, the dance turned into a nightmare. Fitzgerald got drunk, ordered the guests away, and sat alone with a bottle of gin listening to the orchestra. Scottie went home with her friend, Peaches Finney, and Peaches's father. Scottie, though, was nothing if not resilient. Within two hours, she had recovered from her state of near hysteria and was off with Peaches to another Christmas party.

Fitzgerald's earnings for 1936 dropped to about $10,000, and his health did not improve. Shortly after the dance fiasco, he found himself in Johns Hopkins Hospital once again recovering from the ill effects of his alcoholism. In January, he returned to Tryon, North Carolina, staying in the Oak Hall Hotel.

Fitzgerald tried to retain something of a relationship with Zelda. Throughout the summer of 1936, he periodically took her to lunch at the Grove Park Inn in Asheville. They would sit at a table apart from other diners, saying little but behaving impeccably, Zelda often ordering cucumbers in sour cream. Then they might take a walk among the gardens surrounding the Inn. Nervous and unsure what to say, Fitzgerald smoked steadily while he and Zelda sat on a wicker settee to gaze at the mountains.[15] In the spring of 1937, they took a trip together to Myrtle Beach, South Carolina.

One of Fitzgerald's final meetings with Hemingway occurred in June 1937 in New York City. Hemingway was there to give a speech at the American Writers' Congress attacking fascism. Fitzgerald, always ready to help with advice, even if it was not welcome, as it increasingly was not by Hemingway, suggested that Hemingway supplement his forthcoming novel *To Have and Have Not* with some short stories. Hemingway did not take the advice. On June 5, the day after their meeting, Fitzgerald sent Hemingway a short, nostalgic note saying how much he enjoyed seeing Hemingway and wishing they "could meet more often."[16]

Later that month, Fitzgerald was back in New York to discuss returning to Hollywood. He met with Metro-Goldwyn-Mayer (MGM) story editor Edwin Knopf, who recommended hiring Fitzgerald. Increasingly in need of money, Fitzgerald accepted an offer of six months at $1,000 per week. A potential extension sweetened the deal, calling for a raise to $1,250 weekly for an additional year if MGM picked up the option. Yet Fitzgerald must have sensed that time was running short, as he made his will before leaving for Hollywood. He appointed as executors Harold Ober and his longtime Princeton friend John Biggs, Jr., who had recently been named to a judgeship on the Third Circuit Court of Appeals by President Franklin D. Roosevelt as a reward for service to the Democratic Party.[17] Fitzgerald had already grown accustomed to seeking legal help from Biggs, as in his naming Scribners and Harold Ober partial beneficiaries of his life insurance.[18]

With his will settled and a steady income beckoning, Fitzgerald was ready once again to move west. If he thought that he might not have much time left, he would be proven right.

NOTES

1. *The Notebooks of F. Scott Fitzgerald*, ed. Matthew J. Bruccoli (1978; New York: Harcourt Brace Jovanovich, 1980), entry 1034.

2. Matthew J. Bruccoli, *Some Sort of Epic Grandeur: The Life of F. Scott Fitzgerald*, 2nd rev. ed. (Columbia: University of South Carolina Press, 2002), 388.

3. See Nancy Milford, *Zelda: A Biography* (New York: Harper and Row, 1970), 302–04, for a discussion of Zelda's frame of mind at the time.

4. Bruccoli, *Some Sort of Epic Grandeur*, 395.

5. *F. Scott Fitzgerald: A Life in Letters*, ed. Matthew J. Bruccoli (1994; New York: Simon and Schuster, 1995), 285.

6. Bruccoli, *Some Sort of Epic Grandeur*, 400n.

7. *The Crack-Up*, ed. Edmund Wilson (1945; New York: New Directions, 1956) 75.

8. *Afternoon of an Author: A Selection of Uncollected Stories and Essays*, ed. Arthur Mizener (New York: Scribners, 1957), 182. The volume also includes "Author's House."

9. For "The Snows of Kilimanjaro," see *The Complete Short Stories of Ernest Hemingway*, Finca Vigía Edition (New York: Scribners, 1987), 39–56.

10. Sally Cline, *Zelda Fitzgerald: Her Voice in Paradise* (New York: Arcade Publishing, 2002), 358.

11. The relevant letters are available in *The Letters of F. Scott Fitzgerald*, ed. Andrew Turnbull (1963; New York: Dell, 1965), 267, 273, 311.

12. *The Notebooks of F. Scott Fitzgerald*, entry 1915.

13. A portion of the article is available in *The Romantic Egoists: A Pictoral Autobiography from the Scrapbooks and Albums of F. Scott and Zelda Fitzgerald*, ed. Matthew J. Bruccoli, Scottie Fitzgerald Smith, and Joan P. Kerr (New York: Scribners, 1974), 212.

14. F. Scott Fitzgerald, *Letters to His Daughter*, ed. Andrew Turnbull with an introduction by Frances Fitzgerald Lanahan (Scottie) (New York: Scribners, 1965), 6. The volume includes letters from Fitzgerald to Scottie written from 1933 to 1940. The introduction also is informative.

15. Milford, *Zelda: A Biography*, 311.

16. *F. Scott Fitzgerald: A Life in Letters*, 324.

17. For Biggs's accession to the Circuit Court, see Seymour I. Toll, *A Judge Uncommon: A Life of John Biggs, Jr.* (Philadelphia: Legal Communications, 1993), 124–36.

18. *Correspondence of F. Scott Fitzgerald*, ed. Matthew J. Bruccoli and Margaret M. Duggan, with Susan Walker (New York: Random House, 1980), 437.

Chapter 9

TRYING TO RESURRECT THE DREAM: HOLLYWOOD, SHEILAH GRAHAM, AND *THE LOVE OF THE LAST TYCOON* (1937–1940)

HOLLYWOOD AGAIN

Fitzgerald began working at Metro-Goldwyn-Mayer (MGM) in July 1937. He rented an apartment at a hotel named the Garden of Allah and bought a 1934 Ford to drive to work. Although his previous two attempts at screenwriting had brought him limited success, he began this effort with high hopes. His $1,000 weekly salary was good pay for a screenwriter, and he wrote optimistically to Scottie about his expectations of doubling that figure if he could find a way to avoid having his creativity limited by collaborators. The team approach to screenwriting, popularized by Irving Thalberg, was especially difficult for Fitzgerald, accustomed as he was to working alone on his novels and short stories.

Fitzgerald's first assignment was to revise the dialogue for *A Yank at Oxford*, presumably because of his experience writing about university life. The film, starring Robert Taylor and Maureen O'Sullivan, was released in 1938 but retained little of what Fitzgerald had written and gave him no screen credit.

Fitzgerald initially kept his drinking in check during his work for MGM, substituting Coca-Cola. He carried a briefcase full of bottles to work each day and drank steadily, partly because the buildings in which he wrote were warm, but also because the sweet drink helped combat his craving for alcohol.

Shortly after Fitzgerald's arrival in Hollywood, he attended a gathering at the home of actor Frederic March on July 12 to watch Ernest Hemingway show *The Spanish Earth*, a documentary for which Hemingway wrote and spoke the commentary. The film was distributed to raise money for the Loyalists, supporters of the Republican Spanish government who were resisting the fascist insurrection led by Generalissimo Francisco Franco.[1] The event was difficult for Fitzgerald, embarrassed by the downturn of his novelistic career at a time when Hemingway was at the peak of his popularity and unable to afford the $1,000 contribution that Hemingway was requesting from individuals to buy ambulances for use at the front lines.

No account exists of the two men talking with each other at the event, although it is hard to imagine their not greeting each other in some fashion. However, as contemporaries noted, Fitzgerald at the time was increasingly diffident and withdrawn in conversations even with people he had known for a long time. That personality shift coupled with his financial predicament may have been reason enough for him to hang back. Yet a wire from Fitzgerald to Hemingway the following day implies some conversation between them: "THE PICTURE WAS BEYOND PRAISE AND SO WAS YOUR ATTITUDE."[2] This would be the last time the two men, whose lives had been so closely intertwined since the 1920s, would see each other.

SHEILAH GRAHAM

On July 14, Fitzgerald met a twenty-eight-year-old Hollywood gossip columnist named Sheilah Graham. A relationship quickly developed between the two, with Sheilah ultimately fulfilling a number of roles for Fitzgerald: friend, lover, nurse, and something of a supervisor to keep him sober. Her real name was Lily Sheil, and she had been born in a London slum and reared in an orphanage. In her teens, she had married a middle-aged man named John Graham Gillam, under whose tutelage she learned to speak and act in a refined manner. When the marriage ended, she tried her hand at journalism. Although successful with her *Hollywood Today* column, she never reached the level of a Louella Parsons or Hedda Hopper, the queens of gossip columnists.

When Scottie came out to California during the summer of 1937, Sheilah asked to meet her, and the two established a friendly relationship. Scottie stayed with the famous acting couple, Helen Hayes and her husband, Charles MacArthur, and got to meet one of her favorite stars, actor and dancer Fred Astaire.

The interaction between father and daughter did not always go as smoothly as during the 1937 visit. Fitzgerald remained deeply concerned that Scottie not repeat the mistakes he and Zelda had made and seemingly feared that she might inherit her parents' weaknesses. He continued to fill letters with stern admonitions regarding proper behavior and warnings to focus seriously on academics.

After Scottie graduated from the Ethel Walker School in 1938, she successfully applied to Vassar. Fitzgerald, proud of her decision to attend a highly regarded college, gave her a trip to France in the company of Alice Lee Myers, a longtime friend. Both before and after the European trip, Scottie visited her father in Hollywood. Fitzgerald continued planning Scottie's life for her, which she accepted better than most teenagers would. After her matriculation at Vassar, her father wrote, threatening his own apocalyptic binge if she took a drink before she reached twenty. If Fitzgerald could not redo his own past, he was determined to do all in his power to prevent his daughter from following in his own failed footsteps.

THREE COMRADES

Fitzgerald's second writing assignment came from the prominent producer Joseph Mankiewicz: to write the screenplay for the film version of Erich Maria Remarque's novel *Three Comrades*. He eventually was assigned a collaborator, Edward Paramore, but found working with him difficult. Mankiewicz angered Fitzgerald by rewriting their final version; however, the film provided Fitzgerald with the only onscreen film credit he would receive. *Three Comrades* featured an outstanding cast headed by Robert Taylor, Margaret Sullavan (nominated for an Academy Award), Franchot Tone, and Robert Young, and did well at the box office. It earned Fitzgerald a renewal of his contract and a raise to $1,250 per week.

While working on *Three Comrades*, Fitzgerald took time to visit Zelda in early September, taking her and Scottie to Charleston, South Carolina, for several days. The vacation was pleasant and restful, offering Zelda a welcome respite from Highland Hospital and Scottie a rare opportunity to be with both parents at once.

During that fall, Fitzgerald received a telegram from his first love, Ginevra King, saying that she would be in California. After their nostalgic reunion, he called her several times, but they did not see each other again. Later in the year, he accompanied Sheilah to Chicago where she was to do a radio broadcast about films. The trip was marred by a long drinking binge by Fitzgerald. After returning to California, he tried to dry out with the aid of around-the-clock nurses. A January 1938 trip with Zelda to Florida and Montgomery was uneventful, a positive outcome given that Fitzgerald found being with Zelda stressful and exhausting.

The next writing project after *Three Comrades* was a screenplay based on Ursula Parrott's short story "Infidelity." The film was to star Joan Crawford, but the subject matter, adultery, proved so controversial that in May the project was dropped.

One evening during the time Fitzgerald was working on "Infidelity," he and Sheilah went to a performance of his short story "A Diamond as Big as the Ritz" at the Pasadena Playhouse. As Sheilah recalled the event in *Beloved Infidel*,[3] he had long hoped to see the story turned into a play and was excited about attending the performance. Dressed in formal evening clothes for opening night, Fitzgerald and Sheilah arrived in a chauffeur-driven limousine to discover a sparsely attended student production. Nonetheless, Fitzgerald applauded enthusiastically throughout the performance. Afterward he went backstage to congratulate the young actors. On the ride home, though, Fitzgerald fell quiet, contemplating how far his star had dropped since he had been one of the most famous writers in America.

Fitzgerald went back East again in the spring of 1938, but this time the outing with Zelda and Scottie went badly. The three of them took a trip to Virginia Beach and Norfolk, Virginia, during which Scott and Zelda argued about the conditions under which she could leave Highland Hospital, as Scott, fearful of what might happen if she traveled without professional supervision, insisted that a nurse accompany her. Fitzgerald acutely felt not only his financial duty toward Zelda but his responsibility for her welfare and his legal liability in case something went wrong. The argument, as conflicts often did, led Fitzgerald to get drunk.

Upon returning to California, Fitzgerald moved into a house at Malibu Beach that Sheilah had located. The romantic relationship between Fitzgerald and Sheilah was public knowledge in Hollywood, and Scottie was well aware of it. However, there is no evidence that Zelda knew about Sheilah, although she may have surmised that her husband had found someone. Still, both Fitzgerald and Sheilah retained a sense of propriety in their relationship, maintaining separate residences until Fitzgerald's ill health prevented his living alone.

Fitzgerald cared deeply for Sheilah, but the traditional religious values with which he had grown up remained, fostering a sometimes ambivalent attitude toward her. On the back of a photograph of Sheilah, he wrote "Portrait of a Prostitute," perhaps referring to her prior relationships with other men.[4] Yet in his poem "For Sheilah, a Beloved Infidel," Fitzgerald expressed admiration for her beauty as well as appreciation for what she had learned through those relationships. The poem provided the title for Sheilah's own account of her life, *Beloved Infidel*.[5]

COLLEGE OF ONE

Although Sheilah had developed social confidence during her marriage, her formal education had been weak. Consequently, Fitzgerald, who was, as Sheilah wrote in *College of One*, a "born teacher," devised a program of study for her.[6] He created an extensive reading list but also read the books himself and conducted tutoring sessions with her. The curriculum was a two-year program that included literature, philosophy, history, art, and music intermingled with chapters from H. G. Wells's *Outline of History*. Fitzgerald divided the program into courses modeled after a college curriculum, with "Cushman's Philosophy with Readings," for example, a pre-requisite for "Spengler and Modern Philosophers." A career list-maker, Fitzgerald not only prepared a reading list of books but followed it with a "Revised List of 40 Books" and a "Substitute List of Good Novels." He also included a variety of instructional aids, such as a list of literary terms with their definitions. Fitzgerald brought considerable creativity to his efforts at curricular design, for example alternating chapters from H. G. Wells's *Outline of History* with novels.

Sheilah and Fitzgerald called this educational program a "college of one," the title she gave to her book about the experience. While many people might resent loved ones urging massive educational programs on them, seeing the efforts as expressions of dissatisfaction with who they are, Sheilah enjoyed the program immensely. She was intelligent, ambitious, and interested in improving; and the program involved a close collaboration with someone she admired and loved. She expressed her feelings on the matter clearly in *College of One*: "I am immensely grateful that a charming, intelligent man with an inherent magic that could 'illuminate old shapes' decided to give me the benefit of what he had learned from books, and from life."[7]

Fitzgerald moved again in November, renting a house in Encino on "Belly Acres," an estate owned by actor Edward Everett Horton, whose many films included *The Front Page* (1931), *Top Hat* (1935), *Lost Horizon* (1937), and *Arsenic and Old Lace* (1944).

About the same time, he began work on *Madame Curie*, a biographical film about the Nobel-winning scientist who discovered the radioactive elements radium and polonium. The film was intended to star Greta Garbo, but the project was dropped in January 1939, resuming a few years later as a vehicle for Greer Garson. MGM did not renew Fitzgerald's contract again, and he finished his term working for producer David O. Selznick on the blockbuster film *Gone with the Wind*, based on the novel by Margaret Mitchell and starring Clark Gable, Vivien Leigh,

Olivia de Havilland, and Leslie Howard. Fitzgerald's job was to revise the dialogue for the film, using only dialogue found in the novel. As with most of the movies on which he worked, he received no film credit for his efforts.

Fitzgerald earned about $85,000 from MGM during the eighteen months he was under contract. In 1938 alone, he earned over $58,000, his best year ever financially, but a combination of debt, expenses involving Zelda and Scottie, and his own California expenditures left him with little money.[8] Financial need as well as the desire to prove he could make a success of screenwriting led him to seek freelance assignments on films after his MGM contract expired.

WINTER CARNIVAL AND THE DARTMOUTH FIASCO

In February 1939, Fitzgerald started work on *Winter Carnival* for Walter Wanger of United Artists. Collaborating with Fitzgerald was Budd Schulberg, a Dartmouth graduate and son of B. P. Schulberg, who had headed production for Paramount Pictures. Believing that being on location would encourage creativity, Wanger sent Fitzgerald and Schulberg to Dartmouth College in Hanover, New Hampshire, site of the winter carnival that provided the setting for part of the film. They flew to New York and then took a train to Dartmouth. Sheilah was on the same flight, planning to stay in New York and then return to California with Fitzgerald, but perhaps to keep her relationship with Fitzgerald hidden from Schulberg and United Artists she took a seat some distance from Fitzgerald.

B. P. Schulberg had given his son two bottles of champagne, which Budd shared with Fitzgerald, initiating a binge that continued through their entire stay at Dartmouth. During the train ride from New York Schulberg and Fitzgerald got off at a stop and were left behind. They hired a driver to take them to the next station, boarded the train, and continued to Dartmouth. Their drinking continued during the three days at Dartmouth, and Fitzgerald developed a severe cold. Wanger, irate at their behavior, fired both writers (although he later rehired Schulberg), and the two men returned to New York.

Fitzgerald was in such bad shape with a high fever and respiratory infection that Sheilah and Schulberg took him to a hospital. After a few days of hospitalization and another week recuperating in a hotel, Fitzgerald was able to return to California with Sheilah. The film, starring Ann Sheridan, was released in 1939 with Schulberg but not Fitzgerald credited. In 1950, Schulberg published a novel, *The Disenchanted*, based partly on his Dartmouth experiences with Fitzgerald.

Another disastrous trip awaited Fitzgerald in April. One day after an ugly incident during which Fitzgerald became drunk and Sheilah took a gun away from him, he went to Asheville. There he picked up Zelda and continued to Cuba, where he left her in a hotel room while he wandered about Havana drinking. At a cockfight, he tried to stop the roosters from killing each other and was beaten up by the spectators. It remained for Zelda, despite her own illness, to get her husband to New York and into a hospital. Fitzgerald's tuberculosis was found to be active, adding to his problems. During his stay in New York, he took a cab to Harold Ober's house and got into another fight, this time with the cabdriver. Zelda meanwhile took herself back to Highland Hospital. The disastrous Cuba trip was Scott and Zelda Fitzgerald's last time together.

ADDING A SECRETARY, DROPPING AN AGENT

That same month another important woman entered Fitzgerald's life, although not as a romantic interest. Frances Kroll, a young woman seeking a job, found one as Fitzgerald's secretary, signing on for $35 per week. Many years later, she would write a book about her experiences with the famous author during his final year and a half of life.[9]

Her job interview mainly focused on whether she had any movie contacts. Fitzgerald was happy to find that she had none, explaining that he was about to write a novel about the film industry and did not want anyone in the business to know about it.

Fitzgerald was still drinking, but less, and trying to be circumspect. He ordered bottles of gin from a nearby store and had them delivered when his new secretary was absent. In addition to normal secretarial duties, however, Frances Kroll quickly came to assume another task—disposing of his gin bottles in burlap potato sacks so that his landlord would not know of his drinking.

When Fitzgerald was up to writing, he might compose as many as twelve pages longhand a day. Frances would type a copy triple-spaced for easy revising. Then she would incorporate his changes and do a double-spaced draft. Fitzgerald also liked to have her read aloud what he had written so he could hear the sound of the words as well as see them on the page.

Fitzgerald returned to short stories in 1939, revising "Thumbs Up" (published as "The End of Hate") for *Colliers* and, along with other stories, beginning the Pat Hobby series about a hack screenwriter.

The author-agent relationship between Fitzgerald and Harold Ober came to an end in July when the long-suffering Ober finally brought an end to Fitzgerald's habit of borrowing money from him. Surprised, disappointed, and angry over Ober's refusal to lend him more money, Fitzgerald broke off their business association. Ober, though, continued to function as a surrogate father to Scottie, who spent a lot of time, including school vacations, with the Obers.

Scottie broke into print herself that month with "A Short Retort," an analysis of her generation, in *Mademoiselle*. In August, she visited her father in California, where they discussed a novel that Scottie wanted to write and Fitzgerald urged her to take driving lessons in case she might be with a man who had too much to drink. Once again, Fitzgerald was trying to protect his daughter from his own experiences. Over the next year, the tone of his letters changed, as Fitzgerald came to see Scottie as more of an adult and family partner. Scottie in turn wrote wishing that he could come out East to meet her boyfriend, Samuel Lanahan, whom she eventually would marry.

Fitzgerald's novel about the film industry progressed slowly throughout the summer and fall of 1939. His health and need to work on other projects to earn money kept getting in the way. In September, he worked for a week on Samuel Goldwyn's film *Raffles*, starring David Niven as the gentleman thief from the E. W. Hornung stories. Fitzgerald was charged with revising some of the dialogue, a task he had to finish within a week before Niven left to join the British Armed Forces as World War II continued to expand.

Fitzgerald's income for 1939 dropped to about $21,000, and he had to borrow from longtime friend Gerald Murphy to cover the tuition for Scottie's sophomore year at Vassar. In November, Fitzgerald's proposal for *Colliers* to serialize his new novel and offer a substantial advance was rejected. Faced with the disappointment and feeling let down by yet another literary associate, he increased his drinking. One of his drunken acts was to give away his clothes to some men off the street. Had he done that in a sober moment and in moderation, the offering might have been applauded as a charitable act, but that was not the case. Sheilah arrived and ordered the men away. Fitzgerald flew into a fit of rage and threatened to kill her. After she left, he sent threatening notes and stole an expensive fox jacket he had given her.

Fitzgerald came to his senses and mounted a multipronged effort to win Sheilah back. He sent flowers, employed Frances Kroll to deliver an apologetic letter, and largely stopped drinking. By January 1940 they were back together.

THE PAT HOBBY STORIES

The first Pat Hobby story, "A Man in the Way," arrived at *Esquire* on September 16, 1939, as Fitzgerald continued his association with editor Arnold Gingrich, who had published his "Crack-Up" essays.[10] The first Pat Hobby story to be published, though, was "Pat Hobby's Christmas Wish," in January 1940. The stories earned modest but steady financial returns (initially $250, later raised to $300) as Gingrich took almost everything Fitzgerald sent him. The brief stories did not require extensive planning or writing time, and Fitzgerald sent them off rapid-fire. The second arrived only a few days after the first, a third on October 2. Ultimately, *Esquire* published seventeen from January 1940 through May 1941. Even with these brief stories, and despite the speed with which Fitzgerald wrote them, he took his craft seriously, following his initial submissions with second and even third versions. In order to avoid pulling one version at the last moment to substitute another, Gingrich finally sent Fitzgerald a list of issue deadlines for changes.

Hobby is not a likable character. Barely literate and obnoxious, he served not only as a source of money for his author but as a way for Fitzgerald to vent his spleen on an industry that he felt had not treated him fairly—as Frances Kroll wrote, "a punching bag for his own frustrations."[11] Fitzgerald envisioned the stories also being published in book form, and in his correspondence with Gingrich mulled over, steadily revising, the order in which he wanted them arranged. In the collected edition, Gingrich followed Fitzgerald's wishes as faithfully as he could rather than the order of the stories' publication in *Esquire*.

In March 1940, Fitzgerald learned from Dr. Robert Carroll, director of Highland Hospital, that Zelda would be released. The release occurred in April, and Zelda moved to Montgomery to live with her mother. Zelda had improved sufficiently not to require constant treatment, but apparently no one believed that she would ever be completely cured. The improvement pleased both Zelda and Scott; it also removed from him a steady source of expense.

A projected film version of Fitzgerald's "Babylon Revisited" provided another screenwriting job during the summer of 1940. *Cosmopolitan* was to star Shirley Temple as Charles Wales's daughter, Victoria (Honoria in the original story). Fitzgerald earned about $5,000 working on the screenplay, but producer Lester Cowan, who had intended to make the film with Columbia, finally abandoned the project and sold the movie rights for the story to MGM, which made *The Last Time I Saw Paris*

(1954) with Van Johnson and Elizabeth Taylor as Charles and Helen Wills (Wales). Sandy Descher played their daughter, Vicki.

By this time, Fitzgerald had moved from his Belly Acres house to an apartment on North Laurel Avenue near Sheilah's apartment, reducing his monthly rent to $110. His last screenwriting assignment occupied about three weeks from late August 1940 to mid-October as he worked on the Twentieth Century-Fox film *The Light of Heart* (1942), adapted from a stage play by Emlyn Williams. Ironically, the main character, an actor, like Fitzgerald was an alcoholic.

Hemingway's status as America's best known novelist was reinforced in 1940 by the publication of *For Whom the Bell Tolls*. Although Fitzgerald thought the novel inferior to Hemingway's earlier fiction, it sold very well, and Fitzgerald sent a congratulatory letter in response to the inscribed copy he received from Hemingway.

THE LOVE OF THE LAST TYCOON

Fitzgerald, though, had not given up on reclaiming an important place in American literature. By the fall of 1940 he was deeply involved in his new novel. He never finished it and never settled on a final title, although a recent edition is entitled *The Love of the Last Tycoon: A Western*, the title referring not to cowboy-and-Indian Westerns but to the strong and courageous visionary individuals who built the nation and its institutions.[12] Monroe Stahr, the protagonist, a producer of genius fighting an ultimately losing battle against the collective mediocrity and venality of the film industry, is based on Irving Thalberg, who had achieved great early success as a producer and died in 1936 at age thirty-seven. Other characters based partly on real-life individuals include Stahr's deceased wife, Minna (Zelda), and Stahr's final love, Kathleen Moore (Sheilah Graham). Stahr's antagonist is a producer named Pat Brady, whose daughter, Cecelia, narrates much of the story.

Fitzgerald's notes indicate the direction in which he planned to take the story. Stahr, suffering heart disease that would soon end his life, discovers that Brady plans to have him murdered and responds by arranging Brady's murder. On a plane flight, however, Stahr changes his mind and resolves to call off the murder, but before he can do so the plane crashes, killing Stahr.

It is impossible to know whether Fitzgerald would have brought the novel to a successful conclusion, and if so, whether it would have resurrected his reputation as a writer. The general consensus, though, is that the novel showed great promise, and that Fitzgerald had sufficiently managed to control his drinking, with the help of Sheilah Graham, to have a real chance. In Stahr, Fitzgerald certainly had a character that he cared about. For Fitzgerald, Stahr represented a dying breed of heroic individuals who bring to their efforts a romantic readiness to dream greatly. Part of Fitzgerald's attraction to Monroe Stahr, the last of the tycoons, was that he saw himself in similar terms. As he wrote in his notes for the novel, "I am the last of the novelists for a long time now."[13]

FITZGERALD'S DEATH

One afternoon in November 1940, Fitzgerald went to Schwab's Drugstore to buy cigarettes. When he returned, Sheilah could see that he was grayish and unsteady. He admitted that he had become faint at the drugstore. The next morning, he saw Dr. Clarence Nelson, who diagnosed a heart problem and prescribed bed rest. Since Fitzgerald had to climb stairs to his third-floor apartment, he moved in with Sheilah, who lived on the ground floor. Although he spent much of his days in bed, he wrote on a board and gave the material to Frances for typing.

As November passed into December, Fitzgerald's health seemed to be improving, and he was making good progress on the novel. Friday, December 20, though, was a difficult day. Fitzgerald was struggling with a chapter and spent the morning and part of the afternoon in bed. After a mid-afternoon nap, he appeared refreshed and dictated some material to Frances. After she left, he continued writing, making such good progress that he asked Sheilah to call and postpone until the next day his appointment with Dr. Nelson, who was planning to stop by the apartment to administer an electrocardiograph. After dinner, Fitzgerald suggested to Sheilah that they go out to celebrate the day's accomplishments. Sheilah agreed, and they went to see the film *This Thing Called Love* starring Rosalind Russell and Melvyn Douglas.

As the film ended and the lights came up, Sheilah could see that Fitzgerald was ill. She helped him to the car and suggested that they call Dr. Nelson, but in the fresh air Fitzgerald felt better and decided, since Nelson was expected the next day anyway, to wait until then.

Fitzgerald spent part of the morning of December 21 in bed making notes for the novel. Later he got up and dressed. Frances stopped in to pick up mail, and Fitzgerald and Sheilah had a mid-afternoon lunch. When he said that he wanted some ice cream, Sheilah suggested that he not go out to buy it for fear of missing the doctor. Instead, she brought him two chocolate bars. Fitzgerald ate the candy while resting in his easy chair beside the fireplace reading *The Princeton Alumni* and making notes on the Princeton football team. Suddenly he started from his chair, grasped for the mantel, and fell to the floor. Sheilah thought he had fainted and rushed to find a brandy bottle. She poured some brandy between his teeth, but it ran down the side of his face. She tried calling Dr. Nelson but getting no answer tried other doctors and then went to the apartment of Harry Culver, the building manager, for help. As Culver knelt beside Fitzgerald, he saw there was nothing to be done. The chronicler of the Jazz Age was dead.

Fitzgerald, though, had died struggling to right the foundering ship of his career. If the winds of alcoholism, financial difficulties, and changing literary tastes had knocked him off course, he was determined to attempt a recovery. Like his greatest literary creation, Gatsby, he fought on, refusing to give up, keeping faith with the vitality of his dream.

NOTES

1. For an effective overview of the conflict, see Antony Beevor, *The Spanish Civil War* (1982; New York: Penguin Books, 2001).

2. *F. Scott Fitzgerald: A Life in Letters,* ed. Matthew J. Bruccoli (1994; New York: Simon and Schuster, 1995), 332.

3. Sheilah Graham and Gerold Frank, *Beloved Infidel: The Education of a Woman* (New York: Henry Holt, 1958), 215–17.

4. Matthew J. Bruccoli, *Some Sort of Epic Grandeur: The Life of F. Scott Fitzgerald,* 2nd rev. ed. (Columbia: University of South Carolina Press, 2002), 434.

5. Sheilah Graham later revisited the story of her relationship with Fitzgerald in *The Real F. Scott Fitzgerald: Thirty-Five Years Later* (New York: Grosset and Dunlap, 1976). Her son, the mystery novelist Robert Westbrook, later contributed *Intimate Lies: F. Scott Fitzgerald and Sheilah Graham: Her Son's Story* (New York: HarperCollins, 1995).

6. Sheilah Graham, *College of One* (1967; New York: Bantam Books, 1968), 51. Graham includes photographic reproductions of the typed pages with Fitzgerald's hand-written notes outlining the program of study (205–21).

7. Graham, *College of One,* 201.

8. The figures relating to Fitzgerald's earnings are from Bruccoli's *Some Sort of Epic Grandeur.*

9. Frances Kroll Ring, *Against the Current: As I Remember F. Scott Fitzgerald* (1985; Berkeley, CA: Creative Arts Book Company, 1987).

10. Gingrich edited the stories, which were published as *The Pat Hobby Stories* (1962; New York: Scribners, 1995). Gingrich also contributed a valuable introduction to the volume in which he discusses their publication history and his interactions with Fitzgerald.

11. Ring, *Against the Current,* 55.

12. See F. Scott Fitzgerald, *The Love of the Last Tycoon: A Western*, ed. Matthew J. Bruccoli (New York: Scribners, 1994). The volume includes "A Note on the Title," a preface that discusses the projected ending, and about twenty-five pages of "Selected Fitzgerald Working Notes" for the novel.

13. *The Notebooks of F. Scott Fitzgerald*, ed. Matthew J. Bruccoli (New York: Harcourt Brace Jovanovich, 1980), entry 2001. The line supplied the title for Matthew J. Bruccoli's examination of the manuscripts relating to the novel, *"The Last of the Novelists": F. Scott Fitzgerald and the Last Tycoon* (Carbondale and Edwardsville: Southern Illinois University Press, 1977).

Chapter 10

THE COMEBACK: F. SCOTT FITZGERALD'S PLACE IN AMERICAN LITERATURE (1940–THE PRESENT)

Fitzgerald had named Judge John Biggs, Jr., and Harold Ober as executors of his will. After his falling out with Ober, though, Fitzgerald replaced Ober's name on his copy of the will with that of Max Perkins, but Perkins withdrew as co-executor after Fitzgerald's death in order to avoid any possible questions about the legality of his role. Biggs, in fact, began handling arrangements immediately after his longtime friend's death, conferring with Zelda about the funeral and enlisting Frances Kroll's help in having the body sent to Baltimore. Biggs also asked Frances to secure Fitzgerald's possessions and prepare an accounting of his money.

Frances Kroll gathered some of Fitzgerald's clothes that she thought would be suitable for the funeral, including a suit that he had recently purchased from Brooks Brothers, the same company from which he had purchased his military uniform many years before, and with her brother, Nathan, visited Pierce Brothers Mortuary to purchase a coffin. The coffin and other mortuary expenses totaled slightly over $600, a sum covered by the $700 in cash that Fitzgerald had hidden away, sharing its location only with his young secretary. She sent Biggs a copy of the will, a list of Fitzgerald's unpaid bills, a statement of his cash that she had found, and information regarding the transfer of the body, scheduled to arrive during the morning of Friday, December 27, at William J. Tichnor & Sons Mortuary in Baltimore.

THE FUNERAL

A wake to accommodate Fitzgerald's California friends was held at Pierce Brothers in Los Angeles, in the William Wordsworth Room, an appropriate setting for a great writer. One of those in attendance, the writer Dorothy Parker, offered a sympathetic judgment using the words the man with owl-eyed glasses pronounced about the dead Gatsby—"The poor son-of-a-bitch."[1]

In *Against the Current,* Frances Kroll recalls sitting alone in the funeral home with her deceased employer, thinking of his unfinished novel and how Fitzgerald had worried about what she would do for a job when he had completed it.

Over the next several weeks, Frances Kroll continued helping with final details regarding Fitzgerald's possessions, communicating several times with Biggs and receiving letters from both Zelda and Scottie as well as a phone call from Zelda, who expressed appreciation for the help Frances had given her husband.[2]

Zelda was not well enough to attend the funeral service on December 27 at the Pumphrey Funeral Home in Bethesda, Maryland, or the burial later that day at Rockville Union Cemetery in Rockville, Maryland. However, she was closely involved in funeral details and insisted on a large display of flowers. A number of Fitzgerald's longtime friends and associates, however, were present, including the Biggses, Obers, Turnbulls, Murphys, Ludlow Fowler, Fitzgerald's cousin Cecilia Taylor and her four daughters, and Scottie. Rosalind Sayre's husband, Newman Smith, attended, representing the Sayre family. Hemingway did not attend because he was in Cuba and unaware of Fitzgerald's death, and Sheilah Graham stayed away in deference to propriety. An Episcopalian minister, the Reverend Raymond Black, presided at the funeral service. The day was rainy, and after the coffin had been lowered into the grave and covered, Andrew Turnbull's mother laid some pine branches from La Paix on the grave.

Zelda had wanted Fitzgerald buried with his parents, especially his beloved father, at the St. Mary's Catholic cemetery in Rockville. The Baltimore Roman Catholic Diocese, however, refused permission because Fitzgerald had not been a practicing Catholic. It has been erroneously reported over the years that the reason for denying a Catholic burial was that Fitzgerald's books were condemned by the Catholic Church and placed on its list of forbidden books, the *Index Librorum Prohibitorum.* In fact, none of his books was on the list.

Fitzgerald's estate amounted to about $35,000, which Biggs used to provide for Zelda and Scottie. Helping compensate for the small inheritance, Harold Ober, Max Perkins, and Gerald Murphy assisted Scottie with loans so that she could complete her studies at Vassar.

ZELDA AND SCOTTIE

Zelda continued to live with her mother in Montgomery, occasionally returning to Highland Hospital for periods of time. Her remaining years were generally peaceful and productive. She painted a series of watercolors of New York and Paris, did a number of biblical paintings that included not only scenes of Christ's death but also such hopeful images as white doves and butterflies. Her work was well accepted locally with four exhibitions in Montgomery during the 1940s. Zelda returned to other interests as well, creating a new series of historical paper dolls and working on a novel called *Caesar's Things*, which had reached 40,000 words by the time she died. The unfinished novel, like *Save Me the Waltz*, is highly autobiographical and interweaves narrative lines relating to insanity, religion, and a relationship reminiscent of her encounter with Edouard Jozan. She also did her part to help rekindle her husband's literary light, urging publication of his own unfinished novel and speaking to local groups about his writing.

Although Zelda did not attend Scottie's wedding to Samuel Jackson "Jack" Lanahan in 1943, she enjoyed spending time with her grandson, Thomas Addison "Tim" Lanahan, born in April 1946.

Zelda's final stay at Highland began in early November 1947, although it was interrupted by a brief return to Montgomery. In January 1948, Dr. Pine, Zelda's physician, prescribed a three-month program of electoshock and insulin to combat her increasing depression. The treatment led to weight gain and memory loss, but she continued painting and was pleased with the birth of another grandchild, Eleanor Anne "Bobbie" Lanahan, on January 25.

On March 9, 1948, Zelda wrote to Scottie, remarking on the coming of spring and how her treatments were almost over. The next evening, she seemed to enjoy talking with a visitor from Alabama. Later that night, near 11:30, a fire broke out in the kitchen and shot up the dumbwaiter to the fifth floor, where Zelda, having been given sedatives, apparently was sleeping soundly. Zelda was one of nine to die in the fire, all on the top floor. The cause of death was officially ruled asphyxiation. A *New York Herald Tribune* account claimed that both the doors and windows to the top-floor rooms had been locked, making escape virtually impossible, a statement strongly denied by Highland officials. The precise details of what happened that night will likely never be known with certainty. What is certain is that it was a particularly sad end for Zelda, who with her husband had once embodied so much youthful energy, enthusiasm, and talent that they came to represent, perhaps more than any other couple, an entire period of American history, the Jazz Age.

Zelda was buried beside her husband in Rockville Union Cemetery, but in 1975, the diocese having relented, both were moved to the Fitzgerald plot at St. Mary's cemetery. A stone slab in front of the headstone is inscribed with the closing sentence from *The Great Gatsby:* "So we beat on, boats against the current, borne back ceaselessly into the past."

Many students of Fitzgerald may wonder about Scottie and how she turned out given her parents' many difficulties and early deaths. In fact, she turned out very well. Scottie and Jack Lanahan had four children, with Jacky (1950) and Cecilia (1951) joining their slightly older siblings. The Lanahans moved to Washington, D.C., in 1950, and Scottie became deeply involved with politics, supporting Democratic candidates, including Adlai Stevenson in his losing presidential effort against Dwight Eisenhower in 1952.

Scottie became a successful journalist, working for *The New Yorker*, the *Washington Post*, and the *New York Times* among other publications. She also wrote and directed musical revues for charitable causes, such as raising money to combat multiple sclerosis. She attempted but did not complete novels and created but had to cancel a musical about President John F. Kennedy's administration when he was assassinated on November 22, 1963. However, a nonfiction book that she wrote with reporter Winzola McLendon, *Don't Quote Me: Washington Newswomen and the Power Society*, was published in 1970.

Scottie also had her share of sorrows. Her first marriage ended in divorce after twenty-four years, and a second marriage, to Grove Smith, came to an end after twelve years. Scottie's oldest child, Tim, survived service in Vietnam but committed suicide in 1973.

Scottie worked hard to further her father's literary reputation. She donated Fitzgerald's papers and manuscripts to Princeton University in 1950 and contributed introductions to several editions of his writings. During the 1970s, she began to collaborate with Matthew J. Bruccoli on a variety of projects, including *The Romantic Egoists* (1974), which includes a rich trove of photographs, clippings, and other personal documents relating to her parents.

Scottie had once started a memoir, but with four young children occupying her time set it aside. Other concerns intervened, and when she died of cancer in 1986 the memoir remained fragmentary. Her elder daughter, Eleanor, then took up the task, publishing an extensive biography, *Scottie, the Daughter of . . .: The Life of Frances Scott Fitzgerald Lanahan Smith*, in 1995.

FITZGERALD'S LITERARY REBIRTH

Fortunately, the story of F. Scott Fitzgerald did not end with his death or Zelda's—or with Scottie's. Even as Zelda lived out her remaining years, Fitzgerald had been reclaiming the position he had once enjoyed as one of America's brightest literary stars. In fact, he was on the way to achieving a literary permanence that even in his most successful moments he probably could not have imagined. Fitzgerald had died hoping to reestablish himself as an important American writer, but with few reading his books he also knew that his fame and literary reputation might be forever lost.

Fitzgerald's comeback began shortly after his death. Perkins immediately set out to salvage Fitzgerald's final, unfinished novel. He considered having another writer complete the manuscript and approached John O'Hara and Budd Schulberg, both of whom wisely refused, recognizing that no other author could satisfactorily meld with Fitzgerald's unique style. Edmund Wilson, a friend of Fitzgerald's since their Princeton days, agreed to edit the manuscript and put it into a form suitable for publication. Wilson arranged the episodes into chapters, summarized unwritten chapters, and included some of Fitzgerald's notes for the novel. He also supplied a title, *The Last Tycoon*. The novel appeared in October 1941, bound with *The Great Gatsby* and five of Fitzgerald's finest short stories ("Absolution," "Crazy Sunday," "The Diamond as Big as the Ritz," "May Day," and "The Rich Boy"). The volume proved popular and went through five printings by 1948.

In recent years, there has been some criticism directed toward the manner in which Wilson carried out his task. Matthew J. Bruccoli, for example, in preparing a new edition, not only substituted a title (*The Love of the Last Tycoon: A Western*) that occurs in Fitzgerald's papers for the title that Wilson had created but also rejected the ordering into chapters that Wilson had done, substituting "episodes" and "sections" in order to maintain greater fidelity to the unfinished status of the manuscript.

The novel was reviewed favorably, with a number of prominent figures such as James Thurber and John Dos Passos praising it highly. The most prophetic assessment came from Stephen Vincent Benét in *The Saturday Review of Literature*: "You can take off your hats now, gentlemen, and I think perhaps you had better. This is not a legend, this is a reputation—and, seen in perspective, it may well be one of the most secure reputations of our time."[3]

Other volumes came quickly. Wilson edited *The Crack-Up* (1945), an important collection of Fitzgerald's "crack-up" pieces and other essays, selections from his notebooks, and a number of laudatory essays about

Fitzgerald. Dorothy Parker prepared *The Portable F. Scott Fitzgerald* (1945), which includes *The Great Gatsby* and *Tender Is the Night* along with nine short stories that, with few exceptions, are among his finest. Two Armed Services editions, *The Great Gatsby* and a collection of stories called *The Diamond as Big as the Ritz and Other Stories*, appeared during World War II, and Malcolm Cowley prepared an edition containing twenty-eight of the short stories, *The Stories of F. Scott Fitzgerald* (1951).

Clearly a major F. Scott Fitzgerald revival was underway as biographical studies followed these early editions. Arthur Mizener published *The Far Side of Paradise: A Biography of F. Scott Fitzgerald* in 1951, the first major Fitzgerald biography. So much scholarly and biographical interest in Fitzgerald followed during the 1950s that Mizener issued a revised edition in 1965. By then, Andrew Turnbull, who as a boy knew Fitzgerald when the writer rented La Paix from Andrew's parents, had published another major biography entitled, simply, *Scott Fitzgerald* (1962). In addition, Sheilah Graham had written *Beloved Infidel* (1958), about her life before and with Fitzgerald and was to follow with *College of One* (1967), detailing the writer's comprehensive curricular plan for her intellectual and artistic development, and *The Real F. Scott Fitzgerald: Thirty-Five Years Later* (1976), an attempt to explain for later generations what Fitzgerald had been like.

Critical analyses of Fitzgerald's novels and short stories quickly began appearing and have mushroomed over the decades in numbers too great to count. If the large library of books and articles about Fitzgerald covers almost everything from the proverbial A to Z, at least one volume attempts to do so literally: Mary Jo Tate's *F. Scott Fitzgerald A to Z* (1998). A sampling of critical works appears in the book's "Further Reading" section.

Other important early editions of Fitzgerald's writings include *Afternoon of an Author* (1957), a collection of stories and essays edited by Mizener; *The Pat Hobby Stories* (1962), edited by Arnold Gingrich; *The Letters of F. Scott Fitzgerald* (1964), edited by Turnbull; and *The Apprentice Fiction of F. Scott Fitzgerald* (1965), edited by John Kuehl, Fitzgerald having reached the level of importance where even his juvenile fiction was considered worthy of study.

By the end of the 1960s, F. Scott Fitzgerald was securely positioned as one of the nation's greatest writers. In the decades since then, virtually everything Fitzgerald wrote has been published, sometimes in multiple editions. Approximately two dozen volumes have been written or edited by Matthew J. Bruccoli, including *The Romantic Egoists* (1974), the pictorial autobiography that he prepared with Scottie.

Fitzgerald's *The Great Gatsby* became and remains one of the most commonly taught texts in American high schools and colleges. His writings, with *Gatsby* leading the way, have been translated into some three dozen languages. So widespread is interest in *The Great Gatsby* that Azar Nafisi's *Reading Lolita in Tehran* (2003), detailing her clandestine teaching of American classics under the Islamic Republic of Iran, includes a major section on her experiences teaching the novel.

As the twentieth century turned into the twenty-first, a major critical effort was underway to produce a new collected edition of Fitzgerald's writings, The Cambridge Edition of the Works of F. Scott Fitzgerald. About fifteen volumes are projected, including novels, collections of short stories, and essays.

Zelda also was swept up in the Fitzgerald revival. In addition to her novel *Save Me the Waltz*, other writings of hers saw new life in such collections as *Bits of Paradise* (1973), edited by Bruccoli and Scottie (then Scottie Fitzgerald Smith); and *Zelda Fitzgerald: The Collected Writings* (1991), another Bruccoli edition. Zelda also attracted biographers, beginning with Nancy Milford, whose *Zelda: A Biography* (1970) retains its importance even after several other biographical studies of Zelda (and of Zelda and Scott together) have joined it, such as Sally Cline's *Zelda Fitzgerald: Her Voice in Paradise* (2002) and Eleanor Lanahan's *Zelda: An Illustrated Life: The Private World of Zelda Fitzgerald* (1996), which includes illustrations of Zelda's artistic work.

Fitzgerald scholars have much to pore over in addition to published books and articles. Princeton University houses the major collection of Fitzgerald materials, including manuscripts, scrapbooks, photographs, and notebooks. Princeton also has received Sheilah Graham's materials and the Charles Scribner's Sons Archives. Another important collection of Fitzgerald materials, especially published works, the Matthew J. and Arlyn Bruccoli Collection of F. Scott Fitzgerald, is held at the University of South Carolina Thomas Cooper Library.

Several periodicals have been devoted to Fitzgerald. Two of them are now defunct: the *Fitzgerald Newsletter* (1958–68) and the *Fitzgerald/Hemingway Annual* (1969–79). A continuing update of the University of South Carolina collection originated in 1995 and continues: *F. Scott Fitzgerald Collection Notes*. In 2002, *The F. Scott Fitzgerald Review* was born, the effort of a group of scholars also involved with the F. Scott Fitzgerald Society. Since its inception, the society has sponsored eight international conferences as of 2005 along with publishing *The F. Scott Fitzgerald Newsletter*. In Montgomery, Alabama, Zelda's hometown, the Scott and Zelda Fitzgerald Museum invites visitors, especially students, to examine the life of these two talented, tragic, and, for decades now, internationally celebrated people. All of this would be heady stuff indeed for the ailing author who in 1940 was struggling to resurrect his career, fearing that he might be forgotten forever but determined to keep trying.

NOTES

1. F. Scott Fitzgerald, *The Great Gatsby*, preface and notes by Matthew J. Bruccoli (New York: Collier Books, 1992), 183.

2. For reproductions of relevant documents, including the letters she received and the list of bills she prepared, see Frances Kroll Ring, *Against the Current: As I Remember F. Scott Fitzgerald* (1985; Berkeley, CA: Creative Arts Book Company, 1987), 112–28.

3. The passage from the review is readily available in F. Scott Fitzgerald, *The Love of the Last Tycoon: A Western*, ed. Matthew J. Bruccoli (New York: Scribner, 1994), xx.

BIBLIOGRAPHY

PRIMARY SOURCES
Novels

This Side of Paradise. New York: Scribners, 1920.

The Beautiful and Damned. New York: Scribners, 1922.

The Great Gatsby. New York: Scribners, 1925.

Tender Is the Night. New York: Scribners, 1934.

The Last Tycoon. New York: Scribners, 1941. Published with *The Great Gatsby*, "May Day," "The Diamond as Big as the Ritz," "The Rich Boy," "Absolution," and "Crazy Sunday."

Collections of Short Stories (during Fitzgerald's Lifetime)

Flappers and Philosophers. New York: Scribners, 1920. ["The Offshore Pirate," "The Ice Palace," "Head and Shoulders," "The Cut-Glass Bowl," "Bernice Bobs Her Hair," "Benediction," "Dalyrimple Goes Wrong," "The Four Fists."]

Tales of the Jazz Age. New York: Scribners, 1922. ["My Last Flappers," "The Jelly-Bean," "The Camel's Back," "May Day," "Porcelain and Pink," "The Diamond as Big as the Ritz," "The Curious Case of Benjamin Button," "Tarquin of Cheapside," "O Russet Witch," "The Lees of Happiness," "Mr. Icky," "Jemina, the Mountain Girl."]

All the Sad Young Men. New York: Scribners, 1926. ["The Rich Boy," "Winter Dreams," The Baby Party," "Absolution," "Rags Martin-Jones and the

Pr-nce of W-les," "The Adjuster," "Hot and Cold Blood," "The Sensible Thing," "Gretchen's Forty Winks."]

Taps at Reveille. New York: Scribners, 1935. ["The Freshest Boy," "He Thinks He's Wonderful," "The Captured Shadow," "The Perfect Life," "First Blood," "A Nice Quiet Place," "A Woman with a Past," "Crazy Sunday," "Two Wrongs," "The Night of Chancellorsville," "The Last of the Belles," "Majesty," "Family in the Wind," "A Short Trip Home," "One Interne," "The Fiend," "Babylon Revisited."]

Plays

The Vegetable or from President to Postman. New York: Scribners, 1923.

F. Scott Fitzgerald's St. Paul Plays 1911–1914, ed. Alan Margolies. Princeton, NJ: Princeton University Library, 1978. *[The Girl from Lazy J, The Captured Shadow, Coward, Assorted Spirits.]*

Fie! Fie! Fi-Fi! A Facsimile of the 1914 Acting Script and the Musical Score, introduction by Matthew J. Bruccoli. Columbia: University of South Carolina Press for the Thomas Cooper Library, 1996.

Essays

The Crack-Up, ed. Edmund Wilson. New York: New Directions, 1945. Essays, notebook selections, and miscellaneous pieces. ["Echoes of the Jazz Age," "My Lost City," "Ring," "Show Mr. and Mrs. F to Number—," "Auction—Model 1934," "Sleeping and Waking," "The Crack-Up," "Handle with Care," "Pasting It Together," "Early Success."]

Afternoon of an Author: A Selection of Uncollected Stories and Essays, ed. Arthur Mizener. Princeton, NJ: Princeton University Library, 1957. Essays and stories. ["A Night at the Fair," "Forging Ahead," "Basil and Cleopatra," "Princeton," "Who's Who and Why," "How to Live on $36,000 a Year," "How to Live on Practically Nothing a Year," "How to Waste Material," "Ten Years in the Advertising Business," "One Hundred False Starts," "Outside the Author," "Author's House," "Design in Plaster," "'Boil Some Water—Lots of It,'" "Teamed with Genius," "No Harm Trying," "News of Paris—Fifteen Years Ago."]

Anthologies of Short Fiction

The Portable F. Scott Fitzgerald, ed. Dorothy Parker. New York: Viking, 1945. *[The Great Gatsby, Tender Is the Night,* "Absolution," "The Baby Party," "The Rich Boy," "May Day," "The Cut-Glass Bowl," "The Offshore Pirate," "The Freshest Boy," "Crazy Sunday," "Babylon Revisited."]

The Stories of F. Scott Fitzgerald, ed. Malcolm Cowley. New York: Scribners, 1951. ["The Diamond as Big as the Ritz," "Bernice Bobs Her Hair," "The Ice Palace," "May Day," "Winter Dreams," "The Sensible Thing," "Absolution," "The Rich Boy," "The Baby Party," "Magnetism," "The Last of the Belles," "The Rough Crossing," "The Bridal Party," "Two Wrongs," "The Scandal Detectives," "The Freshest Boy," "The Captured Shadow," "A Woman with a Past," "Babylon Revisited," "Crazy Sunday," "Family in the Wind," "An Alcoholic Case," "The Long Way Out," "Financing Finnegan," "A Patriotic Short," "Two Old-Timers," "Three Hours between Planes," "The Lost Decade."]

Afternoon of an Author, ed. Arthur Mizener. Princeton, NJ: Princeton University Library, 1957. See story and essay titles under the heading "Essays."

The Pat Hobby Stories, ed. Arnold Gingrich. New York: Scribners, 1962. See story titles under the heading "The Pat Hobby Stories (*Esquire*)."

The Apprentice Fiction of F. Scott Fitzgerald, ed. John Kuehl. New Brunswick, NJ: Rutgers University Press, 1965. ["The Mystery of the Raymond Mortgage," "Reade, Substitute Right Half," "A Debt of Honor," "The Room with the Green Blinds," "A Luckless Santa Claus," "The Trail of the Duke," "Pain and the Scientist," *Shadow Laurels*, "The Ordeal," *The Debutante*, "The Spire and the Gargoyle," "Tarquin of Cheapside," "Babes in the Woods," "Sentiment—And the Use of Rouge," "The Pierian Springs and the Last Straw," "The Death of My Father."]

The Basil and Josephine Stories, ed. Jackson R. Bryer and John Kuehl. New York: Scribners, 1973. ["That Kind of Party," The Scandal Detectives," "A Night at the Fair," "The Freshest Boy," "He Thinks He's Wonderful," "The Captured Shadow," "The Perfect Life," "Forging Ahead," "Basil and Cleopatra," "First Blood," "A Nice Quiet Place," "A Woman with a Past," "A Snobbish Story," "Emotional Bankruptcy."]

Bits of Paradise, ed. Matthew J. Bruccoli and Scottie Fitzgerald Smith. New York: Scribners, 1974. ["The Popular Girl," "Love in the Night," "A Penny Spent," "The Dance," "Jacob's Ladder," "The Swimmers," The Hotel Child," "A New Leaf," "What a Handsome Pair!" "Last Kiss," "Dearly Beloved." Also stories by Zelda Fitzgerald.]

The Short Stories of F. Scott Fitzgerald, ed. Matthew J. Bruccoli. New York: Scribners, 1989. ["Head and Shoulders," "Bernice Bobs Her Hair," "The Ice Palace," "The Offshore Pirate," "May Day," "The Jelly-Bean," "The Curious Case of Benjamin Button," "The Diamond as Big as the Ritz," "Winter Dreams," "Dice, Brassknuckles & Guitar," "Absolution," "Rags Martin-Jones and the Pr-nce of W-les," "The Sensible Thing," "Love in the Night," "The Rich Boy," "Jacob's Ladder," "A Short Trip Home," "The Bowl," "The Captured Shadow," "Basil and Cleopatra," "The Last of the Belles," "Majesty," "At Your Age," "The Swimmers," "Two Wrongs," "First Blood," "Emotional Bankruptcy," "The Bridal Party," "One Trip Abroad," "The Hotel Child," "Babylon Revisited," "A New Leaf," "A Freeze-Out," "Six of One—," "What a Handsome Pair!" "Crazy Sunday," "More Than Just a House," "Afternoon of an Author," "Financing Finnegan," "The Lost Decade," " 'Boil Some Water—Lots of It' " "Last Kiss," "Dearly Beloved."]

Letters

The Letters of F. Scott Fitzgerald, ed. Andrew Turnbull. New York: Scribners, 1963.

Letters to His Daughter, ed. Andrew Turnbull with an introduction by Frances Fitzgerald Lanahan (Scottie). New York: Scribners, 1965.

Dear Scott/Dear Max: The Fitzgerald-Perkins Correspondence, ed. John Kuehl and Jackson R. Bryer. New York: Scribners, 1971.

Correspondence of F. Scott Fitzgerald, ed. Matthew J. Bruccoli and Margaret M. Duggan, with Susan Walker. New York: Random House, 1980.

F. Scott Fitzgerald: A Life in Letters, ed. Matthew J. Bruccoli. New York: Scribners, 1994.

Screenplays

("N" signifies that the screenplay was not used in making the film or the film was never made; Fitzgerald's contribution varied from film to film because of the standard teamwork approach)

Grit. Film Guild, 1925.

Lipstick. United Artists, 1927. (N)

Red-Headed Woman. MGM, 1931. (N)

A Yank at Oxford. MGM, 1937.

Three Comrades. MGM, 1937–38. (Fitzgerald's only screen credit)

Infidelity. MGM, 1938. (N)

Marie Antoinette. MGM, 1938. (N)

The Women. MGM, 1938. (N)

Madame Curie. MGM, 1938–39. (N)

Gone with the Wind. Selznick International, 1939.

Winter Carnival. United Artists, 1939.

Air Raid. Paramount, 1939. (N)

Open That Door. Universal, 1939.

Raffles. Goldwyn, 1939.

Cosmopolitan. Columbia, 1940. (N)
Life Begins at Eight-Thirty. Twentieth Century-Fox, 1940. (N)

Miscellaneous

Thoughtbook of Francis Scott Key Fitzgerald, ed. John Kuehl. Princeton, NJ: Princeton University Library, 1965.

F. Scott Fitzgerald in His Own Time: A Miscellany, ed. Matthew J. Bruccoli and Jackson R. Bryer. Kent, OH: Kent State University Press, 1971. [Poems, reviews, introductions, blurbs, essays, autobiographical pieces; also interviews, reviews, essays, editorials, parodies, and obituaries written about Fitzgerald.]

F. Scott Fitzgerald's Ledger: A Facsimile, ed. Matthew J. Bruccoli. Washington, D.C.: NCR/Microcard Editions, 1972.

The Notebooks of F. Scott Fitzgerald, ed. Matthew J. Bruccoli. New York: Harcourt Brace Jovanovich/Bruccoli Clark, 1978.

Poems 1911–1940, ed. Matthew J. Bruccoli. Bloomfield Hills, MI, and Columbia, SC: Bruccoli Clark, 1981.

F. Scott Fitzgerald: The Princeton Years: Selected Writings, 1914–1920, ed. Chip Deffaa. Fort Bragg, CA: Cypress House, 1996. [Seventy-four college pieces, including stories, poems, and miscellaneous compositions.]

Selected Individual Stories and Essays by Fitzgerald

Saturday Evening Post Stories

"Head and Shoulders," 192 (21 Feb. 1920), 16–17, 81–82, 85–86.
"Myra Meets His Family," 192 (20 March 1920), 40, 42, 44, 46, 49–50, 53.
"The Camel's Back," 192 (24 April 1920), 16–17, 157, 161, 165.
"Bernice Bobs Her Hair," 192 (1 May 1920), 14–15, 159, 163, 167.
"The Ice Palace," 192 (22 May 1920), 18–19, 163, 167, 170.
"The Offshore Pirate," 192 (29 May 1920), 10–11, 99, 101–02, 106, 109.
"The Popular Girl," 194 (11 Feb. and 18 Feb. 1922), 3–5, 82, 84, 86, 89; 18–19, 105–06, 109–10.
"Gretchen's Forty Winks," 195 (15 March 1924), 14–15, 128, 130, 132.
"The Third Casket," 196 (31 May 1924), 8–9, 78.
"The Unspeakable Egg," 197 (12 July 1924), 12–13, 125–26, 129.
"John Jackson's Arcady," 197 (26 July 1924), 8–9, 100, 102, 105.
"Love in the Night," 197 (14 March 1925), 18–19, 68, 70.
"A Penny Spent," 198 (10 Oct. 1925), 8–9, 160, 164, 166.

"Presumption," 198 (9 Jan. 1926), 3–5, 226, 228–29, 233–34.

"The Adolescent Marriage," 198 (6 March 1926), 6–7, 229–30, 233–34.

"Jacob's Ladder," 200 (20 Aug. 1927), 3–5, 57–58, 63–64.

"The Love Boat," 200 (8 Oct. 1927), 8–9, 134, 139, 141.

"A Short Trip Home," 200 (17 Dec. 1927), 6–7, 55, 57–58.

"The Bowl," 200 (21 Jan. 1928), 6–7, 93–94, 97, 100.

"Magnetism," 200 (3 March 1928), 5–7, 74, 76, 78.

"The Scandal Detectives," 200 (28 April 1928), 3–4, 178, 181–82, 185.

"A Night at the Fair," 201 (21 July 1928), 8–9, 129–30, 133.

"The Freshest Boy," 201 (28 July 1928), 6–7, 68, 70, 73.

"He Thinks He's Wonderful," 201 (29 Sept. 1928), 6–7, 117–18, 121.

"The Captured Shadow," 201 (29 Dec. 1928), 12–13, 48, 51.

"The Perfect Life," 201 (5 Jan. 1929), 8–9, 113, 115, 118.

"The Last of the Belles," 201 (2 March 1929), 18–19, 75, 78.

"Forging Ahead," 201 (30 March 1929), 12–13, 101, 105.

"Basil and Cleopatra," 201 (27 April 1929), 14–15, 166, 170, 173.

"The Rough Crossing," 201 (8 June 1929), 12–13, 66, 70, 75.

"Majesty," 202 (13 July 1929), 6–7, 57–58, 61–62.

"At Your Age," 202 (17 Aug. 1929), 6–7, 79–80.

"The Swimmers," 202 (19 Oct. 1929), 12–13, 150–52, 154.

"Two Wrongs," 202 (18 Jan. 1930), 8–9, 107, 109, 113.

"First Blood," 202 (5 April 1930), 8–9, 81, 84.

"A Nice Quiet Place," 202 (31 May 1930), 8–9, 96, 101, 103.

"The Bridal Party," 203 (9 Aug. 1930), 10–11, 109–10, 112, 114.

"A Woman with a Past," 203 (6 Sept. 1930), 8–9, 133–34, 137.

"One Trip Abroad," 203 (11 Oct. 1930), 6–7, 48, 51, 53–54, 56.

"A Snobbish Story," 203 (29 Nov. 1930), 6–7, 36, 38, 40, 42.

"The Hotel Child," 203 (31 Jan. 1931), 8–9, 69, 72, 75.

"Babylon Revisited," 203 (21 Feb. 1931), 3–5, 82–84.

"Indecision," 203 (16 May 1931), 12–13, 56, 59, 62.

"A New Leaf," 204 (4 July 1931), 12–13, 90–91.

"Emotional Bankruptcy," 204 (15 Aug. 1931), 8–9, 60, 65.

"Between Three and Four," 204 (5 Sept. 1931), 8–9, 69, 72.

"A Change of Class," 204 (26 Sept. 1931), 6–7, 37–38, 41.

"A Freeze-Out," 204 (19 Dec. 1931), 6–7, 84–85, 88–89.

"Diagnosis," 204 (20 Feb. 1932), 18–19, 90, 92.

"Flight and Pursuit," 204 (14 May 1932), 16–17, 53, 57.

"Family in the Wind," 204 (4 June 1932), 3–5, 71–73.

"The Rubber Check," 205 (6 Aug. 1932), 6–7, 41–42, 44–45.

"What a Handsome Pair!" 205 (27 Aug. 1932), 16–17, 61, 63–64.

"One Interne," 205 (5 Nov. 1932), 6–7, 86, 88–90.
"On Schedule," 205 (18 March 1933), 16–17, 71, 74, 77, 79.
"More Than Just a House," 205 (24 June 1933), 8–9, 27, 30, 34.
"I Got Shoes," 206 (23 Sept. 1933), 14–15, 56, 58.
"The Family Bus," 206 (4 Nov. 1933), 8–9, 57, 61–62, 65–66.
"No Flowers," 207 (21 July 1934), 10–11, 57–58, 60.
"New Types," 207 (22 Sept. 1934), 16–17, 74, 76, 78–79, 81.
"Her Last Case," 207 (3 Nov. 1934), 10–11, 59, 61–62, 64.
"Zone of Accident," 208 (13 July 1935), 8–9, 47, 49, 51–52.
"Too Cute for Words," 208 (18 April 1936), 16–18, 87, 90, 93.
"Inside the House," 208 (13 June 1936), 18–19, 32, 34, 36.
"Trouble," 209 (6 March 1937), 14–15, 81, 84, 86, 88–89.

The Pat Hobby Stories (*Esquire*)

"Pat Hobby's Christmas Wish," 13 (Jan. 1940), 45, 170–72.
"A Man in the Way," 13 (Feb. 1940), 40, 109.
"'Boil Some Water—Lots of It,'" 13 (March 1940), 30, 145, 147.
"Teamed with Genius," 13 (April 1940), 44, 195–97.
"Pat Hobby and Orson Welles," 13 (May 1940), 38, 198–99.
"Pat Hobby's Secret," 13 (June 1940), 30, 107.
"Pat Hobby, Putative Father," 14 (July 1940), 36, 172–74.
"The Homes of the Stars," 14 (Aug. 1940), 28, 120–21.
"Pat Hobby Does His Bit," 14 (Sept. 1940), 41, 104.
"Pat Hobby's Preview," 14 (Oct. 1940), 30, 118, 120.
"No Harm Trying," 14 (Nov. 1940), 30, 151–53.
"A Patriotic Short," 14 (Dec. 1940), 62, 269.
"On the Trail of Pat Hobby," 15 (Jan. 1941), 36, 126.
"Fun in an Artist's Studio," 15 (Feb. 1941), 64, 112.
"Two Old-Timers," 15 (March 1941), 53, 143.
"Mightier Than the Sword," 15 (April 1941), 36, 183.
"Pat Hobby's College Days," 15 (May 1941), 55, 168–69.

Crack-Up Essays (*Esquire*)

"The Crack-Up," 5 (Feb. 1936), 41, 64.
"Pasting It Together," 5 (March 1936), 35, 182–83.
"Handle with Care," 5 (April 1936), 39, 202.
"Author's House," 6 (July 1936), 40, 108.
"Afternoon of an Author," 6 (Aug. 1936), 35, 170.

Works by Zelda Fitzgerald

Bits of Paradise, ed. Matthew J. Bruccoli and Scottie Fitzgerald Smith. New York: Scribners, 1974. See story titles under the heading "Anthologies of Short Fiction."

Fitzgerald, Zelda. *Save Me the Waltz*. New York: Scribners, 1932.

Fitzgerald, Zelda. *Scandalabra*, foreword by Meredith Walker. Bloomfield Hills, MI, and Columbia, SC: Bruccoli Clark, 1980.

Zelda Fitzgerald: The Collected Writings, ed. Matthew J. Bruccoli. New York: Scribners, 1991.

SECONDARY SOURCES
Selected Biographies and Memoirs

Buller, Richard. *A Beautiful Fairy Tale: The Life of Actress Lois Moran*. Pompton Plains, N.J.: Limelight Editions, 2005.

Cline, Sally. *Zelda Fitzgerald: Her Voice in Paradise*. New York: Arcade Publishing, 2002.

Graham, Sheilah, and Gerold Frank. *Beloved Infidel*. New York: Holt, 1958.

———. *College of One*. New York, Viking, 1967.

———. *The Real F. Scott Fitzgerald: Thirty-Five Years Later*. New York: Grosset and Dunlap, 1976.

Lanahan, Eleanor. *Scottie, the Daughter of . . .: The Life of Frances Scott Fitzgerald Lanahan Smith*. New York: HarperCollins, 1995.

LeVot, Andre. *F. Scott Fitzgerald*. Garden City, NY: Doubleday, 1983.

Mellow, James R. *Invented Lives*. Boston: Houghton Mifflin, 1984.

Meyers, Jeffrey. *Scott Fitzgerald: A Biography*. New York: HarperCollins, 1994.

Milford, Nancy. *Zelda: A Biography*. New York: Harper & Row, 1970.

Mizener, Arthur. *The Far Side of Paradise*. Boston: Houghton Mifflin, 1951. Rev. ed., 1965.

Prigozy, Ruth. *F. Scott Fitzgerald*. Woodstock, NY: Overlook, 2001.

Ring, Frances Kroll. *Against the Current: As I Remember F. Scott Fitzgerald*. San Francisco: Ellis/Creative Arts, 1985.

Smith, Scottie Fitzgerald, Matthew J. Bruccoli, and Joan P. Kerr, eds. *The Romantic Egoists: A Pictorial Autobiography from the Scrapbooks and Albums of F. Scott and Zelda Fitzgerald*. New York: Scribners, 1974.

Taylor, Kendall. *Sometimes Madness Is Wisdom: Zelda and Scott Fitzgerald: A Marriage*. New York: Ballantine Books, 2001.

Turnbull, Andrew. *Scott Fitzgerald*. New York: Scribners, 1962.

West, James L. W. *The Perfect Hour: The Romance of F. Scott Fitzgerald and Ginevra King, His First Love*. New York: Random House, 2005.

Westbrook, Robert. *Intimate Lies: F. Scott Fitzgerald and Sheilah Graham: Her Son's Story*. New York: HarperCollins, 1995.

Selected Critical Works

Allen, Joan M. *Candles and Carnival Lights: The Catholic Sensibility of F. Scott Fitzgerald*. New York: New York University Press, 1978.

Berman, Ronald. *The Great Gatsby and Modern Times*. Urbana: University of Illinois Press, 1994.

Bruccoli, Matthew J. *"The Last of the Novelists": F. Scott Fitzgerald and The Last Tycoon*. Carbondale and Edwardsville: Southern Illinois University Press, 1977.

———. *Some Sort of Epic Grandeur: The Life of F. Scott Fitzgerald*. 2nd rev. ed. Columbia: University of South Carolina Press, 2002.

Bryer, Jackson R., ed. *New Essays on F. Scott Fitzgerald's Neglected Stories*. Columbia: University of Missouri Press, 1996.

———. *The Short Stories of F. Scott Fitzgerald: New Approaches in Criticism*. Madison: University of Wisconsin Press, 1982.

Donaldson, Scott. *Hemingway vs. Fitzgerald: The Rise and Fall of a Literary Friendship*. Woodstock, NY: Overlook, 1999.

Kennedy, J. Gerald, and Jackson R. Bryer, eds. *French Connections: Hemingway and Fitzgerald Abroad*. New York: St. Martin's, 1998.

Lehan, Richard D. *F. Scott Fitzgerald and the Craft of Fiction*. Carbondale: Southern Illinois University Press, 1966.

Piper, Henry Dan. *F. Scott Fitzgerald: A Critical Portrait*. New York: Holt, Rinehart & Winston, 1965.

Stavola, Thomas J. *Scott Fitzgerald: Crisis in an American Identity*. New York: Barnes & Noble, 1979.

Stern, Milton R. *The Golden Moment: The Novels of F. Scott Fitzgerald*. Urbana: University of Illinois Press, 1970.

———. *Tender Is the Night: The Broken Universe*. New York: Twayne, 1994.

Tate, Mary Jo. *F. Scott Fitzgerald A to Z*. New York: Facts on File, 1998.

Electronic Sources

F. Scott Fitzgerald Society
<http://www.fitzgeraldsociety.org/>
(information about the society, bibliographies, e-texts of selected stories, links to other useful sites)
F. Scott Fitzgerald Centenary, University of South Carolina
<http://www.sc.edu/fitzgerald/>

(essays, biography of Fitzgerald, chronology, information regarding the Fitzgerald
    collection at the Thomas Cooper Library)
Jazz Age Culture Website
<http://faculty.pittstate.edu/~knichols/jazzage.html>
(extensive information on aspects of the Jazz Age, including flappers, cars, the
    Crash of 1929, and many more; various links pertaining to Fitzgerald,
    Hemingway, and other writers of the period)
The Hemingway Society
<http://www.hemingwaysociety.org>
(information on the society and Hemingway)

Biographies of Fitzgerald Friends

Baker, Carlos. *Ernest Hemingway: A Life Story*. New York: Scribners, 1969.

Berg, A. Scott. *Max Perkins: Editor of Genius*. New York: Congdon/Dutton, 1978.

Cowley, Malcolm. *Exile's Return: A Literary Odyssey of the 1920s*. New York:
    Norton, 1934.

Delaney, John, ed. *The House of Scribner, 1905–1930*, Detroit: Bruccoli Clark
    Layman/Gale Research, 1997.

Donnelly, Honoria M., with Richard N. Billings. *Sara and Gerald: Villa America
    and After*. New York: Times Books, 1983.

Elder, Donald. *Ring Lardner: A Biography*. Garden City, NY: Doubleday, 1956.

Meyers, Jeffrey. *Edmund Wilson: A Biography*. Boston: Houghton Mifflin, 1995.

Miller, Linda Patterson, ed. *Letters from the Lost Generation: Gerald and Sara
    Murphy and Friends*. New Brunswick, NJ: Rutgers University Press, 1991.

Reynolds, Michael. *Hemingway: The Paris Years*. New York: Basil Blackwell, 1989.

Spindler, Elizabeth Carroll. *John Peale Bishop: A Biography*. Morgantown: West
    Virginia: University Library, 1980.

Thomas, Bob. *Thalberg*. Garden City, NY: Doubleday, 1969.

Toll, Seymour I. *A Judge Uncommon: A Life of John Biggs, Jr.* Philadelphia: Legal
    Communications, 1993.

Yardley, Jonathan. *Ring: A Biography of Ring Lardner*. New York: Random
    House, 1977.

INDEX

About the Author

EDWARD J. RIELLY is Professor of English at St. Joseph's College. He has published several books on baseball and on popular culture, including *The 1960s* (Greenwood, 2003) and is the author of some 10 books of poetry.